# Thriving on the
# Bipolar Roller Coaster

# Thriving on the Bipolar Roller Coaster

## How To Suceed With Bipolar Disorder

### Phyllis Elliott

iUniverse, Inc.
New York  Lincoln  Shanghai

# Thriving on the Bipolar Roller Coaster
## How To Suceed With Bipolar Disorder

iUniverse books may be ordered through booksellers or by contacting:

iUniverse
2021 Pine Lake Road, Suite 100
Lincoln, NE 68512
www.iuniverse.com
1-800-Authors (1-800-288-4677)

Because of the dynamic nature of the Internet, any Web addresses or links contained in this book may have changed since publication and may no longer be valid.

The information, ideas, and suggestions in this book are not intended as a substitute for professional advice. Before following any suggestions contained in this book, you should consult your personal physician or mental health professional. Neither the author nor the publisher shall be liable or responsible for any loss or damage allegedly arising as a consequence of your use or application of any information or suggestions in this book.

ISBN: 978-0-595-43008-6 (pbk)
ISBN: 978-0-595-87349-4 (ebk)

Printed in the United States of America

# Contents

# Acknowledgments

I am so thankful that I am able to write this book and I know it wouldn't be possible without the love and support of many people. Professionally I want to thank the organization I have worked for these past seven years, Family Ties of Westchester, Inc. They have given me the opportunity to help families and children dealing with social, behavioral and mental health challenges. The richness of this experience has helped me be a better social worker, therapist and person. I want to acknowledge the contributions of all of my clients and their families. It is through their experiences that I have built my knowledge base. I have learned so much from them and have enjoyed getting to know them and watching their successes. I also want to thank the professionals that have helped me through rough times and encouraged me to continue working to reach my goals and live my dreams.

I have been blessed in my life to have a wonderful family and many good friends. To my brother and sister in law, my three sisters and my two brothers in law, I want to thank them for standing in the gap and guiding me . They have always been there, cheering me on. Sharing my life with them has truly been a gift. The friends, Denise, Debbie, Bonnie and Karen have been among my best supporters. We are there for all the good, all the bad and definitely for all the laughs.

Last and most importantly, I want to thank my children, Lisa, Cindy and Andrew for giving me the experience as a mom that helps me pass on my good ideas and eliminate my mistakes. I also have four wonderful grandchildren to enjoy. They are such a joy—they add sunshine and fun always. Then there is my husband, for whom there are no words strong enough to express my love and gratitude. We have been together for 37 years and he has helped me get through everything, from raising our children to getting my masters degree. In my eyes there is no equal. It is all these people who have given me the strength and inspiration to write this book and live my life and my appreciation for them is endless.

# Somtimes Life Is Like That!

My life has always been interesting. There have been many twists and turns, some that I am prepared for and others that catch me by surprise. Bipolar disorder had both elements. At the time that I became most symptomatic my life was very busy. I was in school to become a social worker. I had graduated with my Bachelors' degree and had just been accepted to Fordham University to get my Masters. I had an eight-year-old son and two grown daughters, four grandchildren and a great marriage. Even without school and internships I would have had a full life, but add that in and my schedule was over the top. I went from being organized and purposeful in my daily life to being confused, depressed, manic and overwhelmed. My job at that time was being a counselor at a community residence for mentally ill adults. I loved my work and had a lot of positive beliefs about how all my clients could change their lives. My enthusiasm was contagious and I did see some great results. All of that convinced me that I was in the right place that I had finally found what I was meant to do. I seemed to have an instant connection with my clients who had bipolar disorder. At first, I was just impressed with my "unusual ability" to understand them, and I viewed it as a gift or in more grandiose moments, a talent.

At work I was able to function and do my job but when I was alone at night I was feeling very depressed and scared. It is a sort of tribute to my fierce desire to succeed that the out of control emotions inside me were not detected by my clients, my boss or even my family. At some point I had a conversation with one of my clients and I realized that I was totally identifying with everything she said. When she described her depression and her mania, it was as of she knew me and could read my mind. That should have been a big neon light clue that I was going to have to look at how I was feeling and do something about it. Nevertheless, I held onto a certain kind of disbelief as symptoms took hold of my life. I really felt that I was there to do a job and that I had to be different from my clients. If something was wrong with me I just didn't want to know because I had no faith that the suggestions that I gave to them could also work for me.

I was on intimate terms with depression because I had two severe post-partum episodes and various bouts to a lesser degree over the span of my then forty-four years. I understood the feelings of hopelessness, the lack of enjoyment in life and the constant feeling of deadness inside me. I knew that I was experiencing that but the fact that I was able to maintain my work and my life at home without attracting attention, convinced me that I was still okay. I'd always had some energetic times where I could accomplish an extreme amount of work in a short period of time. I often referred to myself as an "aerobic"cleaner. I was a fast mover, fast thinker and someone who got things done. I always had big dreams and big plans, but nothing that crossed any lines into delusions of grandeur. I had a history of difficulty with sleeping so I didn't think much of it when I missed my first night of sleep. By the time it was a week I was a bit concerned. I was still enjoying the energy, the creativity and the euphoria. I could work on projects and even do some exercise, not something I usually included in my daily routine. The sleeplessness of the past, as symptom of depression, was always followed by a heavy sleep during the day. This time I was awake both day and night and while I was agitated, I wasn't interested in stopping or resting at all. By the sixth week, I was unsure if I would ever sleep again and I was becoming scared because I couldn't control this excess energy. I had continual racing thoughts. Racing thoughts are so disturbing because they often don't connect or they only come in parts, never complete thoughts that made sense. I worked the three to eleven shift at the community residence and when I got home I spent the rest of the night pacing up and down my dead end street and sitting at my computer playing solitaire while my legs bounced up and down.

Through all this my family slept and I let them. I didn't want them to know how I was feeling because I couldn't bear the thought that they would see me any other way, than as the competent mother and wife I had always been. I let two more weeks pass before I was ready to be diagnosed. Instinctively, I knew what I would hear but somehow if nobody said the actual words than it couldn't be true. It wouldn't be official. During this time I continued to work, cook, clean and parent with nobody questioning my ability in any of these areas. I could remain "on" when people were around but when I was alone I was afraid and living in a separate world. I believe my reluctance to tell anyone how I was feeling stems from the years I spent living with my mother who was definitely clinically depressed. My father died when I was fourteen and even though my mother had been depressed before, now she was inconsolable. He was the glue that held her together and I know that she was grieving on top of the depression. At fourteen I couldn't understand the depths of her grief or the symptoms of depression that she lived with daily. No one identified it that way but looking back I can see her sitting in the same chair every day when I came home from school. She would be crying and I would try so hard to cheer her up but nothing worked. I know that when she wouldn't respond I often lost patience with her. If I feel any guilt about the quality of our relationship, it is due to the fact that I had little empathy. I just wanted her to cheer up, something I now know she couldn't do. I couldn't bear my husband or children feeling that way about me.

Despite all the contact I had with people with mental illness, I wasn't educated about the causes. The idea that there must be something I wasn't doing right, never left my conscious thought. I had a kindness that I was able to extend to my clients but I was very judgmental about myself. I held myself to very high standards. I also was watching the lives of my clients and I couldn't envision that my life could resemble theirs. They were in day treatment programs and working part time. I had not yet met people who had bipolar disorder who continued with their plans and dreams and were successful. All of these thoughts and feelings kept me from seeking the help I so desperately needed. The many people in my life that believed in me and my ability to rise above this, deserve much credit for helping me seek treatment and stick with it. They helped me to stay on track with my life plan.

I am at 56, a determined woman, a wife, a mother of three, a grandmother of four a beloved friend, a full time program development manager for an advocacy agency and a therapist at a local clinic, and yes, a person with bipolar disorder. It is last on my list because I refuse to let it define me. My purpose in writing this book is to let everyone know that having this illness makes life more challenging but it doesn't make it impossible. It is my valentine to the people with bipolar disorder that courageously seek to live their dreams, the families that support them and the professionals that continue to try over and over to help. I am in a unique position because I have been alternately and simultaneously, a client, family member and a mental health professional treating clients with bipolar disorder. I have had experiences in all these areas that encourages me to pass my knowledge on. Especially as a treatment professional, I have worked with many people who have bipolar disorder and I know that with help and support they can and do succeed.

My goal is to help clients reevaluate what they can achieve, and family members find hope and coping skills and for professionals to remember to see the person before the illness. The following chapters will address all three groups. I will use what I have learned in my own life and from others I have known and treated. In the world of parenting the saying goes, "it takes a village." In the world of mental health I say, "it takes a team." I hope the insights in this book help all three groups develop the ability to be players on teams whose goal it is to win.

# Is it Bipolar Disorder or Just a Mood?

I remember that when I was taking my first psychology class in college, I thought I had all the illnesses and personality disorders that were described. Depressed, yup I have that, obsessive I always fold my clothes a certain way and on and on. It wasn't just me. The majority of the class was doubting their own and their family's sanity. You could tell by the shocked exclamations of, "I do that, that sounds like me or maybe my husband has this," that it was a universal belief that we were all mentally ill. As we read further, we began to understand that there were different degrees of symptoms and that you had to cross a certain line in order to get a diagnosis and require treatment. Some of the behaviors we were nervous about were just habits, preferences or quirks.

There was a collective sigh of relief when we all got it. I was feeling relieved a little too soon because as time went on it would become clear to me that I had bipolar disorder, not just regular moods. What I had learned in class was good information and it helped me see my symptoms and get treatment early.

In order to have a diagnosis of bipolar disorder, certain symptoms need to be present. Having a bad day and feeling sad or having a really energetic day are not signs of bipolar disorder. Everyone has mood changes, it is the severity and duration of them that separates feelings from disorder. If you are able to function well in your life, except for depression that is situationally appropriate, then it is not a disorder. If your life comes to a halt and you just can't find joy or hope or normal times, then it is more likely to be clinical. I am going to go over the symptoms for both depression and mania with examples, so it will be clear to you where you stand. To have a diagnosis the symptoms have to last most of the day, almost every day for two weeks or longer. You need to have five or more of the basic symptoms to be diagnosed with depression. I had seven of them. I am going to look at depression first.

The most noticeable symptom is having a sad, anxious and empty mood that is not linked directly to a bad experience. There is also a feeling of hopelessness and emptiness that seems to have no end. Things that once were sources of pleasure hold no interest for you now because you can't relate to feeling good. The biggest clue for me is that all my optimism is gone. I have been accused of seeing the world through "rose-colored glasses", always thinking the glass is half full. When I am depressed optimism is a foreign language to me. A country I may have visited but I cannot remember how to get back to. I have a terrible sense of direction and getting lost has been pretty much, a cue to panic. When I am really depressed, I am lost all day, every day. The links I describe later in this book are like finding a map with clear directions that will take me back to a better place.

The first time I knew that I was really depressed was when I was twenty-three. I had just had a beautiful new baby girl, my second daughter, I had a good marriage, friends, healthy children, and I couldn't stop crying or get out of bed. I loved my life but at the same time I felt incapable of living it. I could manage to take care of my children's basic needs but that was all I had the energy for. The trigger for this first major episode was probably caused by post partum hormone imbalance. I had sad experiences in my early years that I had never dealt with. My father died when I was fourteen and my mother died three years later. As a teenager I didn't know how to handle the grief that I felt and no one I knew had gone through any thing similar. I remember just going on and doing the best I could, but when I was twenty-three it caught up with me. One thing is for sure, grief has to be felt, it cannot be denied. I found myself unable to think of anything but my parents and how much I missed them. I have a wonderful family, three sisters and a brother, and we are all very close, but at this time I just wanted to be taken care of by a parent. I think the reality of becoming a parent, maternal head of my own family, made me long for the irreplaceable love that can only come from the people who raised you. At that time, I stayed awake most of the night, thinking and crying. I often would watch my husband and children sleep, always afraid of losing them. I knew that grief is a normal process but it had taken me years to allow myself to feel the pain of the tremendous loss. At a time when I should have been so happy, I was hopelessly depressed. At my husband's urging I decided to see a therapist. These sad feelings went on for eighteen months and nothing seemed to take them away. My therapist was good and caring but in the middle of treatment she left, and I felt abandoned again. At the end of all this time, one day, for no apparent reason the overwhelming sadness was gone and in its place was just a low, manageable, under the surface sadness. I realized that the feeling was familiar because I had felt this low level sadness for most of my life. It is amazing to me that I considered that to be normal because I had nothing to compare it to. Now I had been through eighteen months of unremitting hopelessness and I knew the enormity of depression. Through all the rest of my years I had periods of weeks or months when my symptoms would recur. I had gotten used to it and learned to live with it. From this experience I know that while I had reasons to trigger the depression the devastation on my level of functioning was what changed it from regular depression to a clinical condition. At the time, people who were in this state were expected to talk their way through it. Medication wasn't advanced enough and prescribing it was not common.

Fatigue and restlessness are constant companions when you are depressed. People either can't sleep or they sleep too much. I remember not knowing what I wanted to do. I was too restless to do nothing yet I was too tired to do anything. That kind of confusion definitely leads to another characteristic of depression which is irritability. My husband would take me out and I thought I really wanted to go, but once we left I wanted to go home. When I got home, I wished I was going out. I had so little ability to make a decision and stick with it. My personality is usually to be decisive and clear about what I want and now I never knew what I really wanted. I remember being able to watch my children laugh and have fun and be okay with it, but if I was outside and saw strangers being happy I would be vastly annoyed. I was so irritated by everyday things. My normal temperament is to be agreeable and find humor in life. When I am depressed it is like I have had a bad personality transplant. Nothing is funny, I don't want to deal with everyday life and I just can't decide what to do. I am so tired that it takes all my energy to get through the day and I feel that being involved with other people is too much of a commitment. I really like people, hence, my decision to be a therapist. The fact that I can't deal with them when I am depressed leads to another symptom-guilt. I always feel guilty when I can't do my best, I am lousy company and given the choice even I would hang out with someone else. I also felt guilty about overeating. Some people can't eat when they are upset but for me it is just the opposite. I was gaining weight and I knew for certain that I wouldn't be exercising any time soon. I have treated many people who have made difficulties with food their primary focus. This can lead to bulimia. When an eating disorder is co-occuriirng with depression it becomes really tough to treat.

Many people think of death or suicide when they suffer from depression. I was not so worried about my own death, but I was obsessed with the thought of my family dying. For someone with clinical depression, loss can be a trigger. It can also become an obsessive fear. As a therapist, treating someone with depression, I always explore the types of thoughts they are having. If they are feeling suicidal, I always take that seriously and I insist on them being evaluated by a psychiatrist. I will err on the side of caution. It is human nature to fight to live under even the most dire circumstances. If someone has thoughts of suicide and tells me about them, I know I need to respond not just with empathy, but with action. Sometimes in working with teenagers they will say that they are feeling suicidal but not really mean it. I still don't take the chance and I advise the parents to follow up every threat or thought. Asking if someone is feeling suicidal will not give them any new ideas and sometimes it is a relief for them to talk about it. They can feel supported and safe if they can tell you about these feelings, knowing you will act to keep them safe.

All of these symptoms have a devastating effect on a person's daily life. It is hard to imagine feeling well when you are overwhelmed by depression. I hope that it is clear that having a bad day or feeling a little blue does not come under this category.

While depression isn't fun, mania is crazy. At first there is this incredible increase in energy, which can feel good, especially after depression. The first time I experienced this I just thought I was really being organized and getting a lot done. I felt a zest for life and felt that I could do anything. I seemed to have forgotten that just a few days before I had been incapable of deciding on eggs or cereal for breakfast. I was cleaning out closets and drawers, painting things, moving furniture, all in the same day. I wasn't sleeping and at first I didn't care. I thought, "Oh well, it's just more time to get things done." After a few weeks of this super energy I began to worry that I would never sleep again, and I was becoming less and less organized. I was still moving just as much but it felt like I could never complete anything. When I was up late at night and the house was quiet I would notice that I never actually had a complete thought. I was thinking so fast that I lost track of ideas and plans. A big clue that something was really wrong was when a friend of mine asked why I was talking so fast and so loud. It was a surprise to me because I didn't think I was doing that. When I thought about it, I realized she was right. All of my racing thoughts were spilling out of my mouth and my normal filter was gone. I usually speak appropriately but now I was so speedy that I didn't have time to think before I spoke. The lack of sleep and excess energy and all that thinking was scaring me. I wasn't sure if I would be able to slow down again. I really felt out of control. But enough about me. I want to tell you a story about one of my favorite clients that illustrates a classic case of mania.

Over the years I have talked to and treated many people who are manic. It is easy for me to recognize that incredible speed of thought and speech. There are some symptoms I didn't have but I have seen them many times in other people. To really describe a full manic episode I am going to tell you about someone who taught me a lot. I have never forgotten these lessons, and I have used this knowledge in dealing with myself and others. He was 28, very bright and funny. He was living in the community residence I worked at and I was his primary counselor. My job was to help him learn daily living skills, understand his illness and find ways to cope with his symptoms. He was also a recovering alcoholic and every night after his AA meetings he would stop in the office to talk to me. He would be so intense and ask great questions and during our conversations it felt like he was really getting it. If he needed help with something, I would offer him what I perceived to be pearls of wisdom and his eyes would light up with an "aha" moment. After awhile I started to see the repetitive nature of our talks and it puzzled me. It seemed like we made a good connection but he didn't remember what we talked about. I did some research about bipolar disorder which was his diagnosis, and I realized that he was only getting part of my point because of his racing thoughts. While it made sense to him, at the time, he couldn't recall it later or use it. That changed when he was finally on the right medication but it taught me a lot about how people cope. When he wanted to know something, he just asked repeatedly. I believe he had a sense that our conversations were helpful so he would bring up the same topics over and over and try to make it stick. He had these incredible delusions of grandeur. He was living on a fixed income on Social Security Disability but that didn't stop him from talking a car salesman into letting him sign a contract for a brand new car. When he told me about it, I tried to reason with him. I talked about his limited budget but he was sure that one of his great ideas, and there were many, would come through any day and he could pay for the car. One of his ideas was to have a business where he would sell vitamins, do carpentry, teach tennis and paint houses. If that is not the most manic business plan ever, I don't know what is. He was planning to do all those things for people at the same time. He called it the "I can do anything service." I kept trying to be the voice of reason but with no success. Eventually he became somewhat depressed and able to see that his plans weren't possible. His spending was out of control when he was manic and part of my job was to help him return the numerous things he bought. I tried to teach him how to balance his budget. It was a battle that took a long time for him to win. When he moved out of the community residence and into his own apartment, I was afraid he would be out on the street in no time. Amazingly, with good treatment and medication he managed to live on his own and he still does today. Sometimes I hear from him and he is able to laugh at his "manic business ideas." I want you to know that he has gone on to live an interesting and independent life because even with all his symptoms he never let go of his hopes and dreams. He modified them but he didn't give up on them.

One of the symptoms of mania that has long lasting consequences is combining substance abuse with an already full plate of problems. They use drugs and alcohol to self medicate and because this disorder is about extremes it can take them a long time to understand the damage it is doing to them. By the time they get help for both substance abuse and bipolar disorder their lives have become unmanageable. It is hard for them to find their way back because they are battling two problems. It is important for both disorders to be treated simultaneously because they trigger each other. In looking over literature about dual diagnosis it is found that about 50 percent of people with severe mental disorders get involved in substance abuse. Not all of them are addicted but it comes into play at different points in their lives. When people use substances, they are less likely to seek mental health services and also less likely to follow any kind of treatment plan.

Other symptoms, such as Attention Deficit Hyperactivity Disorder, social anxiety, panic disorders and migraines, often become part of the overall picture. Any of these symptoms, left untreated will cause more frequent and more severe episodes of depression and mania.

If after reading this chapter you feel that you are experiencing some or most of these symptoms, it is time to see a psychiatrist and a therapist. Speak to them frankly about what is happening to you. Everything described here can be treated and managed. It is hard to accept that you may have bipolar disorder, but with good treatment and learning some of the coping skills from this book you can succeed and thrive. On the next page I will list all the symptoms so that you can see them more clearly.

# Symptom Check List

## Depression:

1. A sad, anxious or empty mood that lasts for at least two weeks.

2. Feeling hopeless or pessimistic.

3. Feeling guilty, worthless and helpless

4. Having no pleasure in activities you usually enjoy

5. Decreased energy, feeling slowed down

6. Difficulty concentrating and remembering

7. Difficulty making decisions

8. Sleeping too much or not enough

9. Restlessness and irritability

10. Change in appetite

11. Chronic pain or achiness not related to a physical condition

12. Thoughts of suicide, death or focusing on losses

## Mania;

1.  Sudden increased energy, activity and restlessness

2.  Overly euphoric mood

3.  Extreme irritability

4.  Racing thoughts and inability to concentrate

5.  Talking very fast or very loud

6.  Not sleeping

7.  Unrealistic belief in your abilities and powers

8.  Poor judgement

9.  Spending sprees

10. Risky behaviors

11. Increased use of drugs or alcohol

# Medication and Coping Skills—The Dynamic Duo

I am going to tackle this early because I know that the issue of medication is often emotional and controversial. I remember how scared I was when I understood that I would have to take pills every day just in order to think straight. I had seen the results of medication on people in my family and on the people I worked with at the community residence. For some it was great and for others it seemed to be the curse of their existence. I read books and magazines and anything I could get my hands on to help me make peace in living with a chronic condition. Everything in my life had now become divided into before my diagnosis and after it. I needed to find a new definition of success and to see firsthand people who had the illness but continued to be productive. I read "The Unquiet Mind"by Kay Redfield Jamieson which was encouraging. She had become a doctor of psychology while still in recovery from the harsh symptoms of her early days with the disorder. I read, "A Brilliant Madness" by Patty Duke and I saw that despite her diagnosis she had not only continued to work but she was even able to advance her career. My observations were that attitude had a lot to do with success. People who accepted the treatment for bipolar disorder for what it is had better outcomes in terms of how much they were able to do. People who fought treatment spent their time being consumed with how unfair it was and seemed stuck in the illness. It was like they had gum on their shoes and couldn't move past the problem to see solutions. I knew where I wanted to go in my life and while I felt that it was unfair for me to have to choose medications with side effects I couldn't even pronounce, I was glad it was treatable. I decided that I was going to cooperate with my doctor and therapist and believe for the best. There are things I learned on this journey that I hope will be helpful in your decisions about treatment.

I am a logical person and I wanted to approach my illness with concentration on getting help. I had the great fortune of having a father who taught me that there are solutions if you look for them. He didn't accept defeatist behavior and it was ingrained in me that I had to continue to seek answers. In talking with people I had found that for this medication issue logic was out the window and reality was totally gone. No one seemed to understand the long term consequences of remaining untreated. I did research and my most important conclusion came when I realized that none of this was my fault. I could not be bad enough to cause this illness or good enough to cure it. My behaviors are a result of a chemical imbalance in my brain and are genetically based. Most people seemed to feel that with willpower they could conquer this on their own. Consider this scenario, you go to the doctor and you are diagnosed with diabetes. What are the first questions you ask? Is there medication to take? How can I live a healthy life? Those are normal questions and good responses that show an attitude of cooperation in working with a doctor and a diagnosis to get good results. Few people who are thinking straight decide to see if they can cure themselves by changing their thinking or just by toughing it out. There are many scientific studies on the results of untreated diabetes and it's negative physical effects. Oftentimes, when a doctor tells a patient that they have a mental illness they respond with fear of medication and therapy and a resolve to handle it on their own. These two elements are crucial in overcoming symptoms yet they are hard to embrace. If you look in scientific journals there are studies that show the physical effects of untreated bipolar disorder. It changes your brain. The effects on your daily living in terms of the complications in relationships and jobs or school are enormous and they threaten the entire time line of accomplishments for your life. Knowing that, you may want to consider how to work with mental health professionals that you trust to come up with a treatment plan that you can live with and that will get results.

The first piece of good news is that your condition is treatable. Let that sink in and then investigate the treatments. If you have diabetes no one considers medication and other types of recommended treatments to be optional-something to be rejected if you don't feel like doing it. In the mental health world noncompliance with medical treatments is based in people's ignorance about the physical and genetic basis of these disorders and on the public perception that no real damage is done when people don't receive medical help. I am saying clearly and loudly that—TREATMENT IS REQUIRED-NOT OPTIONAL. If you want your life to resemble anything you want to claim, you need to see that you have to tackle it the way you would any other illness. If you have racing thoughts, mood swings, can't sleep, eat or find pleasure in anything, medical help is necessary. Given the choice I would not say, "keep your insulin, I 'll just have the coma." I can't imagine choosing the chaos of mood swings and racing thoughts over the possibility of living life on my terms. There are neurological tests that show actual differences in the brains of people with bipolar disorder and schizophrenia when compared to the brains of people without these disorders. These are real and scientifically evident differences and when you choose not to take medication you choose to allow your brain to be changed. In these same tests there is clear evidence that people who take medication have significantly fewer differences between their brains and those in the group without the disorders. You still have the right to choose not to get treatment but, why would you do that? There are positive side effects of treatments that need to be explored. Chemical balance is restored to your brain and you are able to make decisions based on clear thinking. You have the ability to maintain jobs and relationships. Life is not like a roller coaster without brakes. Sometimes the side effects of NOT taking medication are lost relationships, lost jobs and broken dreams. For me I have chosen to take medication and any other treatment that will help me live my life in the way I wish to live it.

My own journey to finding the right medication was often difficult. My first visit to the psychiatrist was different than I expected it to be. He encouraged me to talk about my current symptoms as well as my family history. Then he thought for a few minutes and presented me with options. He was very kind and caring and he certainly didn't seem alarmed or pessimistic about my future. He prescribed Prozac and said he would see me the following week. He said I could call him if I had any troubling side effects. I was optimistic that this would work and all this would be done with. I put out of my mind the fact that bipolar disorder is chronic and indulged in magical thinking. Within a week it was clear that the Prozac was making me so jittery that I couldn't stay still at all. I saw the doctor again and he thought we should try Lithium, and he also gave me something to help me sleep. Again I was optimistic and again I was wrong. I had blurry vision, memory lapses and tremors and I felt nauseous all the time. I was doing an internship at the local youth bureau and I kept losing my train of thought. I was having "senior moments" long before I thought I would. I gave it a fair try but soon I knew I needed to try something different. I was getting discouraged because with each new drug I thought I was on the road to sanity, or something close to it. I didn't yet know that finding the right medication is part of the long journey to mental health. I was starting my Masters program at Fordham University and I was still having some very bad days and nights. I did think of not going to school but I have always been persistent and I believed that sooner or later something would work. If not, I could take a break from school then. I was taken off Lithium and we tried Depakote. By that time I had become well acquainted with the daunting list of side effects and I was getting more and more nervous with each new change. I decided to trust my doctor and I gave it a try. By the time my first papers were due I felt significantly better. I found it incredible that I could think again, read and yes, sleep with some success. These were all things I took for granted before but now they seemed miraculous. I was gaining weight which troubled me, but compared to the symptoms that I had just gotten rid of, I felt it was a trade off I could live with. Living with dry mouth was heaven compared to the crazy way I felt when I had thoughts and pieces of thoughts drag racing in my head all day. Sleeping was bliss as was waking up and being able to get out of bed. There have been other medication changes when I have had some recurrence of symptoms, but I have worked on developing coping skills to get me through those times. I have written this because I want to offer encouragement to others who are on this very frustrating journey.

There are definitely side effects when you take medication, some common and some rare. Today any medication you take has a frightening list of these but you need to know that the ones that are rare may only have occurred in a tiny percentage of people. Do some research, don't just take anything. Make responsible and informed decisions. Find a psychiatrist you can trust and one who really listens to you. Managed care has made that more difficult but not impossible. In order to make life work for you it will be important to try new things so keep looking for the health professionals who will care about you as a person and work to help you find the combinations you need to feel your best. Be persistent, read and inquire because you should have enough information to be able to try what is recommended. I suggest that you keep a journal of the medication you take and the effect it has on you. This may become an important document in the course of your treatment. It will help you remember what worked and what didn't and it will help you to give your doctor a clear picture of the course of your treatment.

Medication is an art not a science, so work with someone who is willing to persist until they find what is right. Some practical tips are, be brutally honest when talking to your psychiatrist and stay with current symptoms, not a description of your life from birth. Write questions and symptoms down so that you don't forget what you need to say. Bring someone you trust to take down information the doctor gives you because if you are not at your best you may forget important instructions. I need someone, usually my husband, who will understand the possible side effects and know how to recognize a toxic reaction. I know that it is hard to trust when you are feeling so vulnerable but I believe it is worth thinking about selecting someone to be there for you and assist you with treatment until you are feeling well enough to handle it on your own. Before you rule out medication for good think about these questions. What messes have been created during mania that now need to be cleaned up? Who have you alienated that is really important to you while depressed? Are these situations fixable or do you have to start over for the hundredth time looking for a new job, finding other friends and apologizing to loved ones? If you can relate to these questions because they are a perfect description of your life, the" "no medication" "deal isn't working for you. You can try to give it a time limit such as, "For one year I will take medication the way the doctor prescribes it, then I will judge the results." For that year, try keeping a journal of daily feelings and accomplishments to see if the quality of your life has improved.

If and when it is time to stop your medication you need to collaborate with your psychiatrist so that you don't have bad effects to your body. Here is a classic thing we tend to say. "I am feeling fine so I don't need meds any more." The truth is we are experiencing improved mental health because we are taking them and the chemistry in our brain is more balanced. When I am doing well, I believe that is the time to continue what I am doing because if it's not broken don't fix it. The other common statement that I hear is, "I will look crazy if I take pills." The truth is that your symptoms will be more obvious to people and the disorder will be more noticeable if you don't take the medication. On medication I will make sense when I speak and I won't ramble on with unconnected statements leaving the listener to be searching for an escape from my manic tirade. I won't be so depressed that I can't manage a shower or other grooming necessities. I will be able to listen to people without making dire predictions about, what's the use?, of anything they are trying in their lives. I will have something interesting to contribute to conversations because I will have done more than decide if it's the couch or the bed to stay on today. The medication helps put you on a middle road that makes you function in a reasonable way so that you can choose who you want to tell about bipolar disorder. Without it, symptoms can overwhelm the real you and it will become obvious to even strangers that something is wrong. When I have been manic, I bought a car with no money to back me up, talked my friends ears off and believed that I had accomplished things that I really didn't. When I have been depressed I have no energy to do anything or even believe that I will ever do anything. There are no hopes, dreams or goals, only a heavy black quality to my life. It feels like I am walking uphill under water.

Even when taking my meds there are mood swings, I would be lying to you if I claimed that I am symptom free. I have highs and lows but they are much milder and more manageable. I try not to think of my life in psychiatric terms of mania and depression, so I look at them as days with more energy and less energy. One of the worst symptoms I have is the obsessive thought that someone I love, my husband, my children, my siblings, my grandchildren will die. I can have this thought one hundred times a day on a bad day. I take the scenario so far that I get stuck thinking about it and getting really scared. My husband has joked that if he is ten minutes late I already have my black dress out. I can't conceive that he is stuck in traffic or anything else but dead. It is tortuous. With medication I have more success with controlling this thought process. On good days the thought is like a gnat that I can flick off my shoulder with one finger. On bad days it is like a boulder that I need a team of lumberjacks to remove. Medication has not been a total answer for all the symptoms but it is a step up from that black hole so I can glimpse the light. I can entertain the thoughts that there are possibilities that I can work on. I feel strong enough to take what comes and I have at least the illusion that I can control something in the chaos. I've heard it said that some people believe that medication is a crutch. I believe that it's as much a crutch as a hearing aid for the hearing impaired or eyeglasses that help you read. My medication helps me and no one has the right to stand in judgement about what I need to do to live my life successfully. No one who knows me would even challenge my choice. It's a matter of attitude which makes it a matter of personal choice. If you don't live in my skin, you don't get a vote. We need to take back the course of our treatment and find our own balance. I wouldn't be encouraging you to do it if I didn't know it can work. Some things we try can fail but sometimes the blessing is in what we learn from the trying, which brings me to one of my favorite subjects, coping skills.

I like the word skill because it is something that I can learn. I can practice a skill until I master it. It is something that I have to participate in that will show results. Fighting this disorder gets me nowhere but if I use skills I can manage it. I am not comfortable in the victim role and I get very excited when I find something that I can DO to see myself as capable. Sometimes success has been small, such as taking my head out from under the covers and getting dressed. Other times it is as big as finishing graduate school. The combination of meds and coping skills is a winner. I always say that you can manage your illness or it can manage you. I'm working hard and creatively to be the one in charge. You can learn better ways to cope and acquire the skills you need to thrive with bipolar disorder. That's right I said thrive. Surviving is not enough for me and it shouldn't be for you. Everyone who is still breathing has survived something. We owe it to ourselves to thrive and live life on our terms. No one gets everything they want but everyone deserves to get a healthy portion of what they want.

The kinds of coping skills I will be talking about are what has worked for me and ideas I have gotten from the people I treat professionally. Sometimes symptoms occur even when you are taking your meds because of stress, not getting enough rest, or some traumatic event in your life. Knowing how to deal at those times is essential. I can share suggestions with you but you will have to try them to see if they work for you. One of the things I tell myself when I experience the famous hallmark of this illness, "the mood swing," is that a mood is just that. Get committed to the thought that it will pass and you take away it's power. Sometimes it seems to come from nowhere. I am angry or sad with no apparent cause. I wake up that way, the day hasn't even had a chance to do any damage but I feel as if it has. If I was being logical and making a list of good things in my life, I would find that things are really okay, but I still feel angry or sad. Sometimes this mood will leave just as mysteriously as it came, also for no apparent reason. My life circumstances have remained the same, no big event of great fortune, no winning lottery ticket or significant surprise weight loss. I just feel better. My two post partum depressions passed eventually without medication, so now that I am getting good medical care I will certainly feel better much quicker. I try not to attach heavy significance to my moods or give them the respect of actual feelings that are related to real events in my life. I also check to see if something real has happened. Being sad when it's appropriate and happy at good times is a sign of mental health and I am careful not to pathologize it. I have a good friend with bipolar disorder who has days when his moods change frequently within a day, sometimes even within an hour. Together we have found that if I can distract him or just sit with him the mood will pass. I remind him of other times when this worked and I just help him breathe through it. This used to happen to him frequently but over time, as he stayed on medication regularly and matured in his ability to cope, these episodes happen less and less. One of the greatest coping skills is to build a support team of people who know you well enough to feel comfortable to be involved when you need them. They know enough about you to believe that the mood will pass and enough about your illness to be able to stand with you in times like these. They are people who don't judge and don't underestimate your ability to get through this. They are there when you need them but can back off when you are able to handle things again. There is a wonderful quote that I read that defines friendship for me. It says, "A friend hears the song in my heart and sings it to me when my memory fails." Allow friends to help you and don't isolate. When you feel better you will be the kind of friend you really are and you will help them.

Despite the friends and family who love you, this is a chronic illness and you need a team that includes professionals because you don't want to burn your friends and family out. A good caring therapist definitely has a roll in this area.

Your therapist should be someone you establish a good relationship with. That person should be skilled at helping you work things through. This person is also able to assess what you need. They should be a partner in the search for solutions. Sometimes, when you are feeling well, you can plan with your support system about what works when mood swings hit. For some it is a phrase or a specific action, like taking a walk with a friend who understands. It's important to have a plan or a few plans to chose from because it helps you to move past the mood swing and back to middle ground. I personally don't like anyone to feel sorry for me. I would rather be encouraged to do something and I have a list of things that can help. I want my friends and family to be understanding of where I am at the moment, but able to express strong belief that I can do something to change this mood. Some of the things on my list are, take a walk, take a bath, call a friend, write in my journal, allow myself to take a nap, listen to music and sing even though I know I need to keep my day job because I have no singing talent. These activities raise the serotonin levels in your brain, the feel good chemical, and helps you to affect moods in a natural way. I try to avoid eating mass quantities of chocolate but a small piece can help. I can play a game of computer scrabble, setting the computer player on the lowest level so I get to win. Sometimes I play solitaire because it is mindless and gives me some way to zone out and reduce pressure. Prayer has always helped me because it takes some of the stress of how I can feel better off my shoulders. Spirituality in general, connecting with God as I know him, helps me see hope and comforts me. I try to be grateful for what I do have. I can see, hear, walk-just the basics can help me feel hopeful. Since depression is the antithesis of hope, every way that I can develop hope in myself moves me closer to mental health. Everyone will have their own list of what works. Defining what works for you should be an important project to take on. When I am experiencing periodic depressions, I have determined that I will allow myself some recovery time. I give myself two days to rest, stay home from work and do nothing if that's what I feel like. I always make myself start to do things on the third day because I know that if I let it become a week it turns into a month and so on. I don't want to be stuck so I force myself to do even small things to get moving again. Success breeds success, so as I am able to do the baby steps I start to see myself doing the regular things in my life. Having a vision of where you want to be can help. When I am depressed it feels like I can't do anything and that I never have. I have a written account of what I am capable of in my normal day, and I read that list. I start the process by choosing something off that list that I am determined to do. When I complete something, I find it easier to believe that I can do other things. In taking care of myself I feel worthy of recovery and responsible for replacing negatives with positives. Also, when I am depressed I try to key in on funny movies. Sometimes just seeing someone else experiencing life and finding it funny helps jar me into a better mood. When I can laugh, I know that I will feel better. It gives me hope. Humor has always been a coping skill that has worked for me. When I am down it sometimes takes the form of dark or gallows humor. When I am devoid of the ability to laugh, my family should really be worried. I also always burn food when I am depressed. I used to be a caterer and I really like to cook, but depression robs me of the concentration needed to complete the task. That brings me to another point. Know how to spot symptoms when they are mild and take action right away. If I am burning dinners, I know it is time to examine what is going on with me both mentally and physically. Friends and family can also help at these times because they become my reality check. I can ask them how I seem to them and if my behavior has changed recently. When I am depressed I think that my conversation doesn't make much sense, it isn't cohesive. It is good to be able to ask the people closest to me, who I know will tell me the truth, to let me know if that is happening. I also write in a journal. I find this helpful because when I am depressed I can't remember the good things I am capable of doing. Reading accounts of my successes is evidence that even though I am finding it difficult to get out of bed today, last month I gave a great training on advocacy, or I helped a friend. It gives me the standard for normal behavior that I can achieve when I am feeling well. I like that person who is useful and sometimes reading that journal reminds me of who I really am. I am a person, not an illness.

When I get that extra blast of manic energy, I try to think how I can use it to my advantage. What about that closet I always meant to clean? Are my drawers organized? Since I feel like continually talking, should I take out my long list of people that I need to call and get busy on it? Exercise can be seen as a relief and a way to deposit energy rather than another annoying thing I have to do. The fact is, I am depending on a little manic energy to help me complete this book. When I have racing thoughts, I have had to be really creative in coming up with solutions. It is scary to me and I get caught up in trying to make my thoughts make sense. It is definitely not the way to go. The dots just don't connect. It is usually at night when I have the most difficulty with this symptom. I have tried a few things that give me some relief. One of the things I do is picture a stop sign. I keep looking at it in my mind and as the thoughts race I try to make it bigger, make the letters larger, then smaller, then the color brighter. If I am lucky, by the time I do that I have calmed down enough to fall asleep. These thoughts are hard because even if you fall asleep, you think them right before you go to sleep and you wake up right where you left off. I never feel rested when that happens because my body is stiff instead of relaxed and I am usually moving my legs, even in my sleep. Post medication, this only happens to me under extreme stress such as when I was taking tests and writing papers during my graduate school days. Once it was recognized, I realized that I had always had racing thoughts. They disrupted my sleep at night and my concentration during the day. I always believed that everybody had these thoughts and I was surprised to find out there is a name for them and that fortunately there is help. I discovered all this during a class on abnormal psychology and it validated that it was a real thing not just something I was making up.

Anyway, if the stop sign doesn't work, I pull out the big guns. In my journal I recorded a trip to Mexico that I took where I was in the most peaceful place I had ever known. It was called Xcaret and it had an underground river that I swam in with my family. The water is very cold and clear. There is a gentle current and beautiful fish. Flowers come through the holes in the overhead tunnels. I wrote about it in great detail when I got home because I wanted to keep that peaceful feeling within reach if I needed it. I can get lost in thinking about being there and even if my thoughts don't connect and won't slow down, I can reroute them to a place that I can enjoy being.

On top of these frustrating symptoms came another definition that blew my mind. I knew I had felt like this but I didn't know the name for it. When you are both manic and depressed at the same time, it is called a mixed state. What I call it is a mess. Coping skills are hard to use here because there are no clear feelings and moods can change quickly. If this persists for more than a few days, I suggest that you contact your doctor. More aggressive treatment may be needed until you are stabilized again. I've had this happen a few times and it is really hard to tolerate. I never thought I would be asking my brain to please pick one of these-depression or mania—and consider it a step up to have either. This is one time when I could tolerate the familiar symptoms rather than the unpredictability of the mixed state.

The bottom line here is that you have to determine the quality of life that you want and take the steps to get it. If you feel overwhelmed at taking on the big picture, take it and break it up into manageable pieces. List them in order of priority or just in the order of how you think you will be able to start doing them. It may seem like the to do list is very long but all you are responsible for doing is the next thing on that list. As you accomplish the small steps, you will be able to envision doing more. Don't worry if it takes you longer to do something, we are on a different timetable and once you accept that you won't get discouraged. When choosing a task try to start with something you feel you can accomplish so that you have the advantage of having success. If you take on too much you may fail at it, and while failure is not the worst thing it doesn't encourage you to keep trying. That's right, I said failure is not the worst thing. No one lives life without making mistakes. You can learn from them and I think you need to claim the right to make them. People without mental illness do it all the time and then they just try again. Doctors and family members get nervous if they think we will attempt something that is not a guaranteed success. If I make a bad decision, I just make another decision and try another way. I am not that fragile and I suspect that if you are getting the proper treatment you aren't either. If you knit or crochet, you start with one little row but every time you work on it, it grows and eventually it is a whole scarf. Feeling overwhelmed is paralyzing. When I think of cleaning my whole house, I get intimidated, but if I am going to work on one room or even a part of one room then I can push myself to make the effort. It comes down to us seeing our possibilities instead of our limits. I know that before bipolar disorder I was more able to organize my thoughts and my home. What I have learned is that even though those characteristics are diminished, I can find ways to compensate. My goal in life was never to be the most organized person in the world, it was to be productive and I certainly am that. We can be like the water in the stream, if rocks block its path it goes over them, under them and around them. It's determination and persistence that guarantees success. That's the best coping skill, to try new ways when old ones don't work and to be determined and persistent in believing that we can get where we want to go. In conclusion, I believe that if you seek the combination of medication and therapy and work to develop strong coping skills you can beat the odds and the dire predictions and feel free to move on with your life.

# Education and Advocacy

There is no limit to the amount of education we are able to absorb and there is no limit on the amount of education this world needs about mental illness. We need to know about our illness in its technical terms and we need to understand our symptoms so that we can get the proper help. When I was researching bipolar disorder for myself, I was amazed at the clarity it gave me about what I was going through and also the power I felt by just having that knowledge. I was always asking questions but the answers were too vague and of the "don't worry about it" category. That made no sense to me, I needed to know how to deal with something that was going to be a permanent part of my life. Those half answers had been confusing and isolating but after all the reading I did my illness had been reduced to what it is, a chronic chemical imbalance in my brain, that was treatable.

Education did what nothing else had done so far. It enabled me to see it as a physical illness that was genetic. That relieved me of the responsibility for having it and changed my attitude from one of blame to one of cooperation. I now wanted to learn so I could do more of the good things I was capable of. It seemed like I had been in a jungle of uncut reeds and this had given me a way to cut them down and create a path. I wasn't sure where the path was going but it was better than where I was at the time. Knowing the facts helped me be able to describe what I was going through in terms doctors understood and responded to. I felt like I was able to speak in a way that made medical people treat me with respect. It gave me something productive to do and empowered me to ask for what I needed. I have heard people say that knowing about it makes no difference because there is no cure. I can't agree with that because it was knowledge that guided me from" the darkness of despair to the light of hope." I know that sounds corny, but then depression breeds that kind of sentiment. I remember when watching a Hallmark add could set me off on an afternoon of crying jags. There was nothing too corny for me then. Another really good reason to keep learning and trying to put space between reality and my symptoms.

I read everything I could about people who had bipolar disorder and had done good things with their lives. I read those long lists from internet sites naming famous people who had it and managed to make a substantial contribution to the world despite their disorder. It was reassuring to see that what I was dealing with had not stopped them from being writers, artists, doctors, lawyers, many people from the entertainment field, especially comedians, and even a president or two. They had overcome whatever obstacles presented by symptoms and were able to realize their potential. Their lives had been incredible and that's what I wanted for me. I didn't even have great aspirations. I just wanted to get my masters degree and work with people. I had always wanted that and now I added the goal of trying to impact the systems and the stigma. Nothing too ambitious, a possible and reachable goal. I have always been a stubborn person and now I was going to take that quality and use it to my advantage. If those people could do it then so could I. I also saw the statistics that were negative but if it said that only thirty percent had good recoveries, I was determined that I would be one of those. Instead of looking at the odds and saying I had a 70% chance of failure I concentrated on the positive per cent that had experienced recovery and I identified myself as belonging to that group.

There were many days when I thought that everything was too hard and that persisting had no real value. I was in class and nothing made sense. I came home and everything was overwhelming. I thought if only I just had bipolar disorder to deal with I might be able to do it. But I had a full life that I had constructed with family and friends that I loved and I needed to push to function. I believe that while I had more to contend with, the love of my family and friends and their belief in me made it clear that I couldn't quit. I had too many people I was accountable to. I also had the blessing of having a young son, a bonus child, that kept on making me smile despite depression. If we could bottle what he gave me we could help lots of people and make a fortune. On some days I would be so sad I felt like giving up, but I would look at his face and know I had to keep trying. In my work I have seen that life is hard for everyone. I could not claim that bipolar disorder was more difficult than other problems. When I am working with a client who has cancer, I encourage them to fight. In counseling people with mental illness I encourage them to fight as well. I was talking to other people with mental illness and encouraging them as well. I would be a phony if I couldn't walk the talk. I believed in others' ability to conquer their problems, now. I had the opportunity of believing in my own. On all that sleep challenged nights I read ceaselessly. I was lost on the internet but even in my computer illiterate state I could put in "bipolar disorder" and come up with lots of information. I needed to see good descriptions about how I was feeling and I wanted the science to back it up. I was encouraged by what I read and by the fact that if this much was written about it, I certainly wasn't alone. Even in the dead of night, I could read about other people's experience and identify with them. I could hear about others' journeys, especially those further ahead, and it would strengthen my decision to continue trying with treatment and medication. I could learn how to talk to doctors and what new things were being worked on in laboratories that I had never heard of. It was knowing that people were interested in this disorder that freed me from feeling like I had to create a whole new way of life. Some people had found good ways to live with this and part of my education was to try some of what I read about. That lead me to try some things that didn't work for me but I still learned something from each thing I investigated. I never judge what someone else uses to help them because while all our symptoms are similar we are individuals that need to define what works for us. I began to look at what my needs were and I put time and effort individualizing the steps to my recovery.

I found that there are many levels of education that is needed. We need education for ourselves but families, professionals and the public need it too. It is very difficult for family members to understand how to be helpful and it is up to us to give them at least some clues to reduce their frustration. They had a place in our lives before our diagnosis and now they don't know how to function in that place. They need to know if that place even still exists. Do we want more help, less help or a totally different kind of help? They need to get to a family support group because the people there can relate to their experience and disseminate information to them that will help them feel less alone. While we are absorbed in what is happening to us, we need to realize that it is also happening to them. Bipolar disorder in one person in the family affects every other family member. Parents go from one reality, where they know their child and understand them, to an alternate reality that is totally foreign to them. All the things they thought they were doing right may not fit for the current situation. Siblings may feel left out of the picture as parents deal with the identified patient. If their lives are going well, they may have what is called," survivor guilt." They may wonder why they have been spared. It is hard to talk about good news in a house where everyone is concentrating on doctors, hospitals and meds. They may lose close relationships with their siblings that they treasured and feel a sense of grief. As a matter of fact, the whole family including the person with the disorder, may need to have some time to grieve for the loss of expectations about how things will be for them. When I was at my worst I tried to act as normal as possible but I remember my son asking why I couldn't go to his soccer game. He asked why I didn't think a certain cartoon was funny. I wanted to reassure him that I would be okay but I wasn't sure of that myself. I do know that I made a point of letting him know how special he was to me and that none of this was his fault. How hard it must have been for my wonderful husband and children to know how to do the right thing because the rules had changed and they had no advance warning. I know that when I was living with my mother and her constant depression I would have loved a "how to" guide. I tried everything I knew how to do but I couldn't make her happy. I wish I knew that it wasn't something I had done wrong that made her feel so bad and that I wasn't responsible for fixing it. I tried to make that clear to my husband and my children because on top of my feeling bad I didn't want the guilt of making them feel responsible in any way for what was certainly not their fault. Families need to support each other and become knowledgeable about this illness so that they can help when we need them to and so that they can feel empowered to walk with the confidence that only comes when you know that there is hope of treatment and recovery.

Professionals in all spheres need to become educated about mental illness. If you are not a psychiatrist or therapist, you still need to know how to handle situations that may arise. I have two situations that come to mind. I went to my dentist and I was filling in the requested information and I had to list my medications. Of course I listed the psychiatric meds along with vitamins just like they asked. The dentist asked why I was taking Wellbutrin, Trileptal and Alprazolam and I told him it was because I had bipolar disorder. His reaction was really something. He started to talk louder and slower. It was like he thought in that two minutes between the time he read the chart and now, I had become deaf and stupid. I was taken aback but I decided to ask him why he was behaving like that. He said that he didn't want to upset me and he looked a little afraid. I was upset and I proceeded to explain to him that I was raising a family and worked full time and that my symptoms were under control, thank you very much. He was embarrassed as he should have been and apologized and I let him off the hook. It's really hard to find a good dentist. When he left the room the hygienist told me that she had bipolar disorder but had never told anyone about it. I encouraged her to get past her feelings of shame and gave the names of books and web sites where she could get information. The only reason the dentist had the reaction he did is because he was ignorant of the facts. It would have been good if they had taught him something about disorders he might encounter in his practice as a required course. But since they didn't I took that opportunity to pass on what I know and to raise his awareness. He either listened and got the message or he didn't. At the very least I stuck up for myself and took a small step toward combating stigma. The second incident occurred when I was working in my capacity as a professional. I had a client who needed a hospitalization and I was with him in the emergency room waiting for him to be seen. He was very anxious and it took the doctor on call a long time to get to him. When we were in the hall after her less than thorough examination she said to me, "I would rather deal with the physical, these mental ones drive me crazy." She said it in a conspiratorial tone that implied we were on the same page with that feeling and she was close enough for the patient and the family to hear her. We not only were not on the same page, but we weren't even in the same book. She was quite shocked as I informed her how ignorant her statement was. I told her that she should be competent to care for people with any kind of illness and that she should certainly be respectful of the patient and his family. She still didn't seem to feel that she had done anything that was out of line. I finished the admission and then I went home and wrote a formal complaint to the hospital. The administrator called to apologize and I said he needed to do that to the patient and family. Then I expressed my disappointment that the staff was not more prepared and I offered to do an in service training for them. He said that it was a good idea but it never happened. Those two experiences may seem negative but they just put a spotlight on the need for us to understand what we deal with and pass along what we know. I also want to state that I have met wonderful, caring people in the mental health field who have helped me tremendously. We need to search out these people and when they do something good we need to let others know. A letter of thanks to the person with a copy to their supervisor can go a long way in letting them know that their efforts and their competence is appreciated. We can get angry at the reactions that I described in my two experiences but it makes it clear that we need to know about our illness so that we can speak up and educate the ignorant. Sometimes I get tired of doing that and I wish that they would all just "get it" but then I see an ad for awareness about cancer or aids and I know that this is all just a process of informing people so that they can "get it and do something about it." If we just get angry and refuse to speak out no one will spend the money to do the research that will bring about the cure we hope for. No one will know that the stereotypes are wrong or that statistically there is no higher numbers of violent acts for people with mental illness than there is for people without it. The reason the incidences seem so high is that it always is reported as a prominent fact by the media if a crime occurs. Which brings us to the issue of stigma. Stigma occurs when the public perception about an issue is negative. It has to be supported by media and general ignorance to survive. I love that the National Alliance for the Mentally Ill has a web site called Stigma busters. It has people that watch the news, magazines and other entertainment venues for negative statements or stories about people with disorders. It then confronts them and sends educational information to them. Sometimes it works and sometimes it doesn't. I am just glad that it exists. When I read, hear or see something that reinforces a negative stereotype about mental illness I go out of my way to correct it. I have a great sense of humor but I don't find jokes about our pain any more acceptable than I do racist jokes. I believe that even with mental illness we have to maintain the ability to laugh at ourselves, but it is different when it comes from someone outside our situation and it portrays us as less than we are. Our best defense against stigma is to live our lives well and make it known that we do. Anyone looking at our lives should understand that we may struggle but that we are contributors with a place in this society. I hope that it is now clear to you why we need education for ourselves, our families, the professionals that work with us and society as a whole. If each of us does our part things will change in time.

Another issue for us is advocacy. How can we get what we want? How can we be treated sensitively and fairly? I believe this is a place where families can get involved. When we are at our most vulnerable, we may not be able to speak up for ourselves. If our families know what our rights are they can be our voices. If they know that everyone should have a comprehensive discharge plan upon leaving a hospital they can help start the process. They can make sure you are involved in all decisions concerning you. When we are feeling well, we can discuss what we want in our lives so that when they talk to providers they will be able to make suggestions that accurately reflect what works best for us. We should know all about the Patient Bill of Rights and what a Healthcare Proxy is. We should know about the confidentiality laws and know what we want shared with our families and what we want to keep private. I suggest that you consider that any information that is needed for your family to help you, such as facts about medication, options for treatment and places to get treatment in the category of non confidential. As we recover, we need to look at how to advocate for ourselves. I've seen and heard so many negative statements made to people with bipolar disorder that I am wary of letting other people set up limitations for me. I've heard doctors say, "He'll never work again, or drive again or go back to college." The person that they are seeing who isn't used to taking these medications, or is spacy and tired is not who you will always be. You will be able to do more and more as you recover and I believe that saying that you will,"never" do something is not true or fair. It is important to understand that all those things can be a part of your life in time. We need to know that we may not get to do everything we want right away but with time and patience and hard work we will get a job, drive a car, go to college. It took me three years to get my masters degree and other people did it in two years. I needed to accept that it would take me longer without giving up and saying," what's the use." I did get it and it has helped me get where I want to go. Keep your eye on the big picture. We need to be realistic about what our plans are but we shouldn't accept blanket statements about our abilities from anyone. Whether it is professional, family or friend, I just won't accept predictions that don't allow for my unique spirit to rise above my symptoms. You need to ask people to stay away from the word never. When can I try to do that again? How can I work on getting ready to work, drive or anything else again? Ask for help in being creative about achieving the things you want do. Be responsible for setting your own limitations. Don't push to do so much that you set yourself up to fail, but continue to try to take small steps on a daily basis to head in the direction of your goal. Remember that you have an absolute right to have goals and dreams and to work to get to them. It is up to you to take responsibility for where you end up and for the life you create.

The last place you need to advocate for yourself is a very important one. You need to advocate in society to change unfair treatment and stigma. You need to know which way political officials vote on mental health issues. You can find this out by going onto the web site of the National Alliance for the Mentally Ill, (www.nami.org). You can make informed decisions about whether or not laws that are trying to be passed will be helpful to you and others with mental health disorders. There are ways to let people in the congress and senate know what you think should happen by calling their offices and telling them. It is a simple process. You get the number of the bills that you want to talk about and call the number, simply stating that you are for or against it. If we all do this, we can have an effect on what happens in our country on this issue. We can start to leave a legacy for the next generation that will offer them better health care. We will show that our opinions can make a difference in getting someone elected and that will give us some lobbying power when we need it. Other illnesses have large lobbies and voter campaigns and I believe it's time for us to have one too. If we don't stand up for ourselves in the political arena, no one else will. We are worth it, we are contributors to society and we deserve fair treatment. Insurance and budget cuts have determined the quality of our treatment for too long. It is time for us to take a stand and let everyone know that we are strong advocates, a force to be reckoned with.

# Recovery and Hope

For many years, the word "recovery" was never used in connection with mental illness. It seems that everyone else could expect recovery and that there were "steps" and timetables to accomplish it. If you have surgery, the doctors and nurses can't get you moving towards recovery fast enough. They have you on your feet and they are devising a plan on how to keep you there, how to help you adapt to any new challenges you will face. Adaptation to your situation is very important because even though your life has changed you still have to find a way to live it and to make it as close to what you originally wanted it to be as possible. If you have mental illness, you are in the time warp where you just never know how you will feel or how long anything will take. Instead of having a schedule for starting to return to life as you used to know it, you operate in a vacuum of vague and somehow mysterious predictions. Nothing is certain when you deal with any illness but it seems as if mental illness is it's own kind of "Never land." You are there and you have no idea when you will be allowed to leave. It has been apparent to me in places that I have worked that maintenance is the goal, not recovery. When I try to push for more creative discharge plans or more activities for my patient, I am considered a "troublemaker" and not realistic. We need to have solid step by step plans about how we will adapt to our illness and create new lives. Your caretakers, professional and otherwise, may have questionable faith about what you can do and when you can do it. You, the only person with direct knowledge about what you are ready to try doing, are often the last person that is consulted. The most important thing to know is that recovery is possible and you have a right to expect it. You also need to know that it doesn't happen if you don't believe it can. When other people can't grasp the concept that we will do productive meaningful things again it is our job to convince them that we will do just that. We will do it slowly and carefully, but make no mistake, we will do it.

The only way to live with chronic illness is to keep a clear picture of what we want our lives to look like in the forefront of our minds. We deserve to reclaim our lives by adapting to our illness. We can't let bipolar disorder rob us of dreams. To recover means to bring our life back to a semblance of what it was before we had our symptoms, before hospitalization or decompensation. It means to restore order where there is chaos. Sometimes, because of what we learn while we are ill our perspectives change and we can even experience an improved life using the knowledge we have picked up along the way. I think that after we start doing what is medically required to begin the recovery process we need to commit to figuring out what we can do to restore our life. The professionals are right to advise us to do things gradually because the timetable for our recovery is slow. A big mistake that many people make is that they have unrealistic expectations about what will happen when they start treatment. People think, "I am taking my meds so now I can do anything." It is true that taking medication is a good start but it takes time for the drugs to have the full effect. Therapy is good but it also takes time to sort out what has happened to you and how to proceed. We need to be realistic about what we can accomplish and how long it will take to do it. All this while maintaining a positive attitude. No big deal, right? Wrong, it is a very big deal and not easy to do. It seems that if you have bipolar disorder your life isn't about, "easy", it's about possible. We can wallow in the unfairness of it all or we can set about the task of finding meaning and joy in our lives again. I think everyone wallows for a little while but then you just have to pick yourself up and work on the things that will help you get on with life.

I have heard doctors make dire predictions about whether people will work again and I have seen the downcast faces of clients who believe that the doctor is always right. I am here to tell you that I know for a fact that many of those people have gone on to prove the professionals wrong. In my twelve years of working I have attended two graduations, one from college and one from a young girl who received her masters in social work. Both of these people were told that they couldn't do this but yet they did. I have seen people return to work and take on many challenges. There are many success stories that don't get enough representation in the press. We always hear about the person that didn't take meds and ended up homeless and possibly violent. I am here to tell you that this upsetting picture is the exception, not the rule. We can achieve what we want to and in the process we will change the public perception from one of hopelessness to one of figuring out "when" we will recover not "if" we will. It is something we have to do for ourselves with support from our team. The best way for people to help us is to believe along with us that we have capabilities and strengths and that success is within reach. If we can see it, we can make it happen. Our limits should always be self imposed, something we decide on.

We also need to be aware of language we use when referring to ourselves. I have bipolar disorder but I am not bipolar. The difference is that the first phrase says that I have something but the second one says that I am something. I will admit having the disorder but not to being it. The difference may seem like it is just a matter of semantics but I believe that it is connected to the image we hold of ourselves. That image determines how far we can go and how much we will try. This point was driven home to me when I was working in the community residence. I worked with a thirty-year-old man who had schizophrenia. He had been given the diagnosis when he was in college and I know that he had insight about what is was and how it was affecting his life. At one point he read a pamphlet about schizophrenia and the description of the illness and the permanency of the outcome predictions were overwhelming to him. He kept saying "I am just a schizophrenic." This statement was so disturbing to me because I had known him for two years and I never thought of him in those terms. To me he was a gifted poet, a sensitive and caring individual, a person with a good sense of humor and somewhere down the list I acknowledged that he had schizophrenia. Nothing I said could stop him from believing what he had read and from giving it more importance than the evidence of the independent life he had created for himself. I wanted to help him get past this and so I used his favorite form of expression. I wrote him a poem. I put it on his bed and hoped for the best. He read it and he promptly criticized my ability to write a poem, which was encouraging. He was starting to see that just because I wrote that poem it didn't make me a poet and that just because he had this particular set of symptoms it didn't make him "just a schizophrenic." He went on to accomplish many things in life that people had said weren't possible. He was able to see firsthand that he could still have a productive life. At the end of this chapter you will find the poem I wrote for him.

Collectively I have seen clients buy houses, get jobs, go to school and build lives. They are defying the predictions and to me that is worthy of being front page news. In my own life I have accomplished lots of things. Although I experience symptoms on a daily basis, I make the decision every day to do what I am capable of doing and to be who I was meant to be. It is not easy but it is rewarding. People who know that I have bipolar disorder often forget that fact about me or are surprised by it when I refer to it. I want to change the stereotype by the example of my life and by bringing to light the many other positive stories of success that exist. The good stories stay under the radar but now it is time for us to thrive and to make it known. I am going to write about eight links to recovery that I have found. You may know of more and I hope that you will contact me if you do but if you feel lost and without a plan I hope that you will try these suggestions.

The first link is to do a written positive self assessment. I know I am always talking about writing things down, but I know that if my mind is racing the thoughts I have committed to paper will remain the same. They can be my map and guide back to where I want to be. In this positive assessment we will look at what we can do, not what we can't do. Sometimes it is hard to come up with the positives because we are used to the negatives. I always had a harsh tape of criticism playing in my head from the words my mother used to say to me. There was no delete button and they came there unbidden, automatically whenever I needed to face a challenge. When I was raising my first child, I had so many doubts about my abilities as a mother that I often thought that she would be better off with someone else. I couldn't connect with why my husband wanted to stay with me, by choice and very lovingly. I felt that friends must stay out of pity. As I write this, I realize that this is the relatively narcissistic. I wasn't overly invested in success but I was consumed by keeping all these negative images alive. Instead of focusing on what I could give to others or even on just believing the good things they said about me I was stuck in the quagmire started by my mother but continued by me. My mother was long dead and those tapes were still number one on my hit parade. Where she had stopped, I had picked up. She only had material for the eighteen years she knew me but as the years went on I picked up many more mistakes and failings to add to the foundation she laid. No one would ever be as hard on me as I was. Some of the thoughts were just bad habits I fell into, places my mind went automatically. Changing a bad habit requires work and dedication but what could be worth more than building a self image that allows me to have success in my life. I had accomplished a multitude of things in many places, I had made some very good decisions but I couldn't seem to stop my bad self image. By the time I figured out how to see myself in a better light I had raised three children and they were doing well. I somehow never got the point that I was doing well, achieving goals and being a good contributor to life. I had the national malaise, "low self esteem." I think that all the experiences that we have with bipolar disorder reinforce the negative. We need to search for the best in ourselves. I have always had friends and family that loved me but I was blind to the fact that I was lovable. Look at the people in your life and really try to see what they see in you. One of my favorite things to do when I am getting down on myself is to go to my special box of cards, notes and letters that I have saved over the years that express how others feel about me. There are work commendations, good school and work evaluations, cards from family and friends and notes that testify to the fact that no matter how bad I am feeling about myself, other people don't agree with me. I can't be right and all of them are wrong. When I need a boost, I do that and usually halfway through my box I think I'm not really that bad, in fact I might be pretty good. My newfound definition, after much soul searching, of self esteem is the buildup of right decisions. These successes give you the confidence to try things and to expand your view of life's possibilities. Use the worksheet at the end of this chapter to help you see your good qualities clearly. Please read the questions on the work sheet and answer them honestly. There is also a card that you can carry around in your wallet to remind you of your strengths.

Think of the many ways your life affects others positively. If you get stuck for examples then think of how you would like to affect others positively. If you are in a rut try to do one small positive thing a day to increase your sense of purpose and to add to the positive thoughts you can have about yourself. Carry the answers to the questions with you and read them twice a day to reinforce how valuable you are to yourself and others. It will be much harder to say and think bad thoughts about yourself if you do this. After awhile your habits will change and it will feel funny to go back to that dark place where you live in and believe the negative. Nowhere on this list should there be a reference to what you can't do. It is not useful or productive to dwell on those things. It creates a defeatist attitude. We will not be blind to the fact that we aren't perfect but we will use our strengths to minimize our faults and solve problems that previously overwhelmed us. If the list is small keep adding to it as other people say nice things about you. And by the way, when people compliment you, just say thank you and allow yourself to experience pride in that accomplishment. I don't know you but I can start off your list by saying that you have spirit and determination because you are reading this book in an effort to better your life. You are persistent, not a quitter. If you are getting up every day, you are strong and everything you accomplish during the day shows that you are capable. If you are feeling really bold, you can ask others that are close to you to help you with this list. Start your own special box and make it a point to keep cards and letters that express people's positive experiences with you. I know that you can see yourself in the best light and that it will help you recover.

The second link is to "recognize your symptoms. We cannot afford to allow symptoms to persist for long without us taking action to counteract them. Keeping our heads in the sand will not benefit us. If you start to feel the level of your functioning slipping you need to take notice and use the coping skills you have learned. When we wait too long, we get too far into it and feel that we can't get out. When you are experiencing a symptom, how does it feel? What is the first thing that happens or how does your thinking or mood change? One way of becoming aware of the beginning of symptoms is to notice if people are reacting differently to you. Another is to examine your day. Did you overreact to something small that wouldn't affect you at other times? I find that I am less tolerant of noise and crowded places when I am symptomatic. What I do for that is give myself a break from being in situations that will be noisy and crowded for a few days. I gradually allow myself to try to be in places like the mall for short periods of time to test whether my tolerance has increased. If it hasn't, I take another short break and then I try again. I refuse to accept that I can never be in places that are noisy or crowded because that would limit my life in ways that I can't accept. I have a friend who is very anxious in social situations. For a long time he would just avoid these experiences so he was less anxious but the downside was that he was very lonely. We talked about it and we devised a plan for him to go to nonthreatening places such as a movie first and to work up to places where one to one contact was more possible. It was tough and it took a while but eventually he was able to meet some people he could trust and enjoy. He found a hobby and a place to meet others who shared this interest. I remember the night he called me and told me about the first time he went to a club devoted to his hobby. He was nervous before he went but he persisted, based on his past successes in the gradual efforts to increase his tolerance for social interaction. He had so much fun that once he was there he forgot that he has social anxiety. This helped him continue to try things. It is not that he never has a bad experience but that he has allowed himself to have enough good times to draw on that encourages him to be bold enough to change the boundaries of his life. It is okay and even necessary to acknowledge the symptoms we have but it is very rewarding and exciting to discover ways to keep them from limiting our lives. Our recovery depends on how introspective we will allow ourselves to be and how honest and insightful we can become about our true selves. We need to keep a standard for functioning that is clear to us and use it as a guide to help us see when we need help. We have to do this without questioning every little thing we think or do. That's why it is good to create a standard that is reasonable. I have said before that if I can't sleep or I start to burn the food it is time for me to see what is going on. I have recognized what happens at the beginning of an episode and defined it. Try to define what happens when things are starting to go downhill and what is helpful to get you past that point without lowering your regular functioning. People without bipolar disorder have bad days too. We don't need to put everything we say and do under scrutiny but we need to have a general awareness of where we are, a kind of emotional temperature. If you have a cold or flu and your body temperature is 102 degrees you take notice and get the right help. You probably don't take off work or go to bed if you sneeze a few times a day or cough a little. This is just like that. Know when what you are feeling is just a sneeze or if it is the equivalent of a bipolar flu and take care of yourself accordingly. I am not at the mercy of a mystery disease, I know it well and because I am familiar with its characteristics I can be more comfortable in dealing with it.

The third link is one we have talked about before so I just want to mention it briefly. We need to take care of our mental health with appropriate treatment. It is important that we recognize the value of good treatment and make it a part of our regular health routine. We also need to be mindful of our physical health. When we get sick physically, we will be more vulnerable to increased symptoms. We need to sleep well, eat well and get some extra sun and exercise. These are things that everyone needs but they will be important links to our ability to recover. It is hard to add the regularity of good health habits if we feel scattered in our minds but it becomes a kind of circular problem if we don't. No sleeping, eating, exercise leads to poor physical health which leads to poor mental health which makes it hard to pay attention to the details of maintaining good physical health and so on and so on. It's a cycle that we have to break with conscious and conscientious effort. Sometimes I have the hardest time even looking at what I need to do because I get caught up in the various moods I go through and I just don't feel like caring about it. It becomes important to me when it is obvious that my symptoms have gotten the upper hand. Then I race to get back onto my good plan with varied results over a period of time. Sometimes I just don't feel better fast enough and want to give up. Then I go back to my written plan for my own health. On it I have listed how much sleep I need, what a good diet is for me, when I should eat, what kind of exercise can I tolerate, when to take meds and vitamins and when to see my doctors for regular exams. I have devised this written plan so that I have something concrete to work with. When I read it, I feel as if I don't have to start from square one, like for a change I am prepared. Sometimes it is overwhelming to me to make all the changes I need at the same time so I pick a place to start and work my way up. I remember a time in my life before bipolar disorder when I was more organized and more able to regiment my life. Now it just doesn't come naturally, but if I work on it I can still get there. I can sleep a reasonable amount, remember to eat at regular intervals instead of skipping meals and to exercise enough so that I feel myself approaching health. I am never perfect in these things but I suspect that many people in all circumstances have that problem. I just know that the consequences for me will be an increase in symptoms that will make reaching goals harder. Maybe none of this was as important when I was younger but then again maybe I just didn't notice. All I know is that now it is obvious to me that maintaining my physical health has to be a priority.

The fourth link is to pull together a good support system. It should have people who love and respect you and it should be formed using all the areas of your life. There are family members who you can be close to, friends you can make and keep, work buddies, people from church and neighbors. If you try your best to be the kind of person who is a good friend when you are well, others will stick by you when things are hard for you. If that hasn't been your experience in life, you need to look at what part you play in relationships that have gone bad. The symptoms of bipolar disorder do not include rudeness, continual irritation and bad temper, and complete self absorption. Every relationship needs both parties to participate. If the other person does all the giving, all the time, sooner or later they will walk away. If you are taking good care of yourself your capacity to have good, committed relationships with people will increase. When you are well, you have the capability to care and to be fun to be with and to express concern for others. Go out of your way to be interested in their lives because that is part of being in a relationship. It will help you in many ways because it is mentally healthy not to focus on yourself exclusively. Despite the challenges we face, it can't always be about us. Tap into your compassion, your humor, your creativity to make time spent with you something to be cherished.

I love my family because they don't treat me differently, they expect me to pull my weight. Unless otherwise informed they take it for granted that I will be there for them and do what I have always done, which is take care of them. It has been my privilege and my joy to be a wife, mother and grandmother and I know that they can see that it would always be the desire of my heart to be who they know me to be. To make them laugh, to listen to them and give my brand of welcome or unwelcome advice, to do activities with them and to confront them when needed is the standard of my relationship with them and I try to reach that standard whenever possible. They certainly are understanding if I need them to be but they are not condescending or patronizing. They appreciate the good and they would do what I need them to when I am not at the top of my game. My friends have been wonderful and I am always thankful to have them. They offer me a chance to laugh, vent, talk and do normal things. They would notice if I was too depressed or manic and they would be honest enough to tell me. I can count on them and they can count on me to give them the best I've got when I am well. I also try to stay attuned to current events so that I can be part of their conversations. If I am talking to them and it becomes a monologue instead of an exchange of ideas, I know that I have to broaden my focus. One time when it was particularly noticeable that mental illness can take over someone's life was when I was working with a young man during the 9/11 attacks. As a clinician I had been prepared for him to be upset and I had thought through how to help him with this trauma. He was so self involved that he barely knew it had happened. He said that it didn't affect him at all. He felt that his life was so bad that it didn't matter what happened in the world. He was unsympathetic to the victims and could only focus on himself. That astounded me. I had a difficult time with how disconnected he was. As a clinician I always encourage my clients to expand their life views by looking at world events and by reading things they can discuss with others. When most people ask how you are they are looking for the generic "okay." The saga of every feeling you've had this week will not be an appropriate answer and it will certainly keep them from asking again. There are times when we need to be free to really say how we are but sometimes we need to ask and genuinely want to know how someone else is. Taking our minds off ourselves can be a good way to start to feel better.

At work I have let people know that I have bipolar disorder but I don't expect them to make enormous accommodations for me. I try to do my work the best I can and when I need a break, I use sick or personal time. I know that if I needed them to change something in order for me to be able to continue working while dealing with symptoms they would. My support system works for me because I love these people and I give them my heart with trust that they will be there for me. Trust your instincts about the people you choose to be a part of your life and don't expect to never get hurt. Sometimes people can disappoint you but you need to be flexible enough to know that they have lives and issues of their own. Their inability to be there for you at a particular time is not a personal affront to you but rather a byproduct of their own life circumstance. All relationships have ups and downs, look at people's hearts and always believe they have good intentions unless they have repeatedly proven otherwise. The support system you put together will add substance, meaning and joy to your life.

The fifth link is having the ability and the vision to set goals. Goals add structure to your life. They are the equivalent of a road map. If you leave your house to go somewhere you've never been before and you don't take any directions you might get there or you might get hopelessly lost. Life is like that too. There is a saying that goes, "he who aims at nothing will surely hit it." We all had plans before bipolar disorder and now we need to look at them again and revise them as necessary, but never abandon them. Goals need nurturing, they need patience, planning, time and effort to accomplish, but most of all they need a plan. Before you put together a list, think about what you value and what values are important to you. Your goals should reflect who you really are and what kind of life you want to create. Prioritize, prioritize, prioritize! Do some soul searching, a kind of values assessment. Look for your passions and see how they can be included in your everyday life. Will they lead to satisfying work? Will they just help you feel good? Are they fun? Do these activities that are connected to your passion suggest how to fill in your road map? This map may not look like the maps of friends and family. The roads won't be as straight and there will be detours but the satisfaction upon reaching the destination will be the same no matter how we get there. If we stop because it is too hard, or seems too far away, we may miss some of the most exciting and rewarding experiences of our lives. We need to make long and short term goals. Short term goals are good for giving you the confidence to plan long term goals. As you have success reaching a goal, you will be able to enlarge your vision to include more ambitious tasks. Each of your goals need to be broken up into manageable pieces. We need to take daily steps to accomplish what we ultimately want. As long as we move forward, or continue to return to our chosen path if we have a setback we will prevail. We will see the opportunities and we will take advantage of them. When I went back to school my ultimate goal was to be a licensed social worker. I had to go to school for seven years to accomplish that. I needed four years to get my bachelors degree and three to get my masters degree. I had licensing tests to take and internships to do. If I couldn't break my major goal into small ones, such as just finishing a paper or studying for a test, I would have been overwhelmed and I never would have completed my schooling. I love what I do now and I love the life I have created but it wasn't done with a giant leap but with many, many small baby steps. There were times when I couldn't believe how tired I was and how much there was to do. When I took statistics I felt like I had entered a foreign country. Everyone spoke the language but me. It was very discouraging and I thought I should give up. Then I determined that I couldn't let that stop me. I had to just bear with it so that I could finish it and move on to other subjects that were interesting and useful to me. If I gave up, I would be so disappointed today, and lost because I let myself be cheated of my dream. Sometimes the road to our goal will be filled with unpleasant tasks, things we don't understand, times when giving up seems attractive. At those times we turn to our supports to encourage us to keep going. Every step gets you closer and all the things you do to get where you want to be can teach you something. Everyone spends time doing things they don't like such as laundry, dishes, being stuck in traffic, but we should figure out what percent of our time goes to the activities that are important to us. Do I love doing laundry? No—but it helps me meet my goal of looking well. Evaluate if what you are doing is part of the process of reaching your goal. If it is, just count it as necessary and do it. One foot in front of the other is the best way to get where you are going. Keep a positive attitude and don't get bogged down in complaining. Be grateful that you have the ability to persevere and recognize the value in what you are trying to do. There will be steps on the way to the ultimate completion of a goal that will be tedious but if we keep a steady vision of where we are going we will get there and it will be rewarding. At the end of this chapter I will include some worksheets on goals and some steps to accomplish them. Use them and enjoy the satisfaction you will have when you begin to set your own course in life. Other people's goals for you may not take you where you want to go but your ability to set them for yourself will be the important step to having the life you want.

The sixth link is work. We all need to have meaning and purpose and our daily schedules need to reflect that. There is value in any activity that gives you pleasure and a feeling of belonging in the world. Work doesn't always refer to paid employment. All the years that I was a stay at home mom, I worked very hard. There was no paycheck for what I did but the results have been priceless. I know many people with different disabilities who find ways to work. Some volunteer and some find jobs or careers that are satisfying and fulfilling. In order to make choices about what you want to do you need to think about what you believed you would do before you became caught up in this illness. There was a before and sometimes the answers for now reside there. I have some examples of ways people that I have worked with have created opportunities to do work that was meaningful to them. One young man I worked with owned an old car and he was always working on it. It was so clean that you could eat off it. It was the best it could be and he was his happiest when working on it. After many tries at other jobs it occurred to us that he should try to use his talent and passion for cars. He found a job at a car dealership and he detailed and cleaned new cars before they were picked up by their new owners. The people that got the cars he worked on were lucky because he put his heart into it. He enjoyed the job and was able to stay there for a few years, far surpassing his previous ability to stay with a job. His recovery was amazing during that time because he was doing something that required him to be able to work to his capacity. I know a woman who had tried many jobs and while she was always a good worker, she just hadn't found her passion in life. At some point she started to study gardening and she could barely contain her excitement about her superior ability to grow plants and flowers. Her work was so creative and expressive. She researched her subject and before long she started to work on other people's gardens. Her work is excellent, her new company is booming and she has found a way to live out her passion while making a good living. There was also a client of mine who was thirty-five, had schizophrenia, was able to work part time at a supermarket but never felt fulfilled. We explored what his dreams were and he finally said that he had always wanted to play professional baseball. He became really animated when he spoke about this and I could see that he needed to try to do something about this. I knew that his age and other factors would probably not be in his favor in a professional situation but I didn't discourage him as he researched the ins and outs of spring training and becoming a part of a team. He came to the conclusion on his own that he couldn't do this and he was quite disheartened. I suggested that he see if he could play for a local team. We talked about how to deal with his symptoms in possible situations that could come up if he made it onto a team. Then we looked into all the neighborhood teams and how to get on them. He was so nervous when he went to the tryouts but he was elated when he made it onto the team. He practiced hard and he loved everything about the sport and his team mates. They appreciated his obvious enthusiasm, and, by the way, he was a really good player. I used to love to see him practice and I had the privilege of going to his games to cheer him on. He won the Most Valuable Player award that first year and you would think he had won the Nobel prize. He didn't make any money but he fulfilled a dream and added a new dimension to his life. There is a wonderful young man that I know who has bipolar disorder but he also has a dream. He wants to be in the armed forces. He has looked into it and he knows how demanding it will be, but he also knows that he wants the opportunity to try. As I write this he is in Afghanistan. He was able to meet all the challenges and reach this goal. At first thought it seemed like an impossible plan, given his symptoms and his diagnosis. As time has gone on I have seen him find ways to adapt and compensate and be successful in doing it. I am betting on this being a life changing experience for him no matter what the outcome is . In all these situations the people reached just a little farther than they had before. They believed that they could do something more and that they could change. The common bond was that they had found their niche. Everyone has something special to offer the world. Everyone is unique, and if you miss the chance to share your gifts and talents with the world around you something that could have been will never be. It is sad for you if you don't look for the gifts and the passion you possess, and it is sad for the other people who can benefit from your contributions.

Statistics show great improvement in the lives of people with disabilities who contribute in some way. For all other disabilities there is an expectation that the person will adapt to their challenges and do meaningful work. We need to raise the bar and require more of ourselves. There are many days when I wake up depressed or exhausted by my out of control thoughts and I want to stay home. I know that if I give in I may end up not being able to get out of the rut, not doing what I was meant to do. If I can just get out of bed and put one foot in front of the other I can get to work and once I am there I will get absorbed in the process of what I do and very possibly forget to be depressed. If I stay home in bed I will definitely not forget about it, I will dwell on it and give it the opportunity to increase. Instead of the small gray dot I saw in the morning when I didn't want to get out of bed I will see a big black ominous cloud. I need to live with purpose. If I couldn't do my job I would have to find something else to do. I would visit a nursing home, cuddle an AIDS baby, dish food out at a shelter, anything to keep my life from losing value. I know so many people with bipolar disorder and when I look at them I see passionate, funny, intelligent beings with plenty to offer. My frustration comes when I see that they are afraid to use what they have. They have accepted the limitations of professionals, family and society and stopped looking for the possibilities. Some of these people are my friends and family, not my clients. They have enriched my life in so many ways that I can't imagine my life without them. Society needs your passion and your contributions. Work, both paid and unpaid, will help you connect to your own value as a person and will take you further in your recovery than you can imagine.

The seventh link is acceptance. You can fight it, deny it, but it won't do anything but make you more frustrated. This is a place where the principles of the Serenity Prayer can be of help. This is a prayer used at Alcoholics Anonymous meetings and it contains great insight on how to live with any chronic condition. It says, "God grant me the serenity to accept the things I cannot change, courage to change the things I can, and the wisdom to know the difference." When you are diagnosed there is fear about what can happen to you and also grief for what you believe you have lost. Everyone has some ideas of how they want life to go. I always thought I would graduate college, get married, have children, buy a house, then have a fascinating career. That was my time line when I was in my teens and each event had an age attached to it. A time I had to accomplish it by. I have done all those things but certainly not in the order I planned them. I graduated high school as planned. I got married and got pregnant right away, before I had the house that I had thought was a prerequisite for starting a family. I graduated from school at age forty seven, a good twenty years later than I planned. While on the way to my desired career, I made several pit stops at jobs that were necessary but not satisfying. At the time that I was diagnosed I had again mapped out my plans for graduate school and work and other things. I find that when my mind races I plan and plan and plan, so I was pretty much scheduled from there to death when bipolar disorder came along to interrupt my schedule. At first I was determined to push through but it soon became apparent that it would be impossible. My reaction was that it was all or nothing. I hear this so often in my practice from clients at the beginning of this journey. If I couldn't do it according to plan then it just wouldn't happen. I never looked at the many ways you can accomplish a goal. I had extreme tunnel vision. I was angry at this roadblock and for a while I believed that I couldn't go further. I felt my life was spoiled and I felt heavy with the concept of disability. I saw myself in such a negative light that other people's encouragement felt like it was false. They were just saying it because they didn't know what else to say. I felt like my brains had turned to mush and my motivation was gone and my carefully planned life was soon to follow it. I had many positive people in my life, a great therapist and a wonderful psychiatrist and a husband who never gives up on me. I sometimes found myself annoyed at their statements because they were not the ones going through this. As the medication started to work I could think a little clearer and things seemed possible, maybe. Not definite, just possible. I was in school trying to get through it and at home I was trying to take care of my responsibilities. It was so hard. I never felt like I had sufficient energy yet somehow I was making the effort. I often thought that it was too much and why should I try so hard. I've said before that I am stubborn but in this case it was working for me. While I was feeling less than adequate to do what I was doing, I had to persist in trying. I had goals and dreams and if I couldn't accomplish them it wouldn't be because I had not tried. Throughout this time period my self esteem plummeted. I didn't tell many people outside my family that I had bipolar disorder so I had to pretend I was okay for the majority of the time. It was good because it made me work to appear normal and that showed me that I could at least look like I was functioning. It was bad because I acted as if nothing was wrong and so much was expected of me, all of which I did at the expense of my physical and mental health. I always felt as if I was holding on by the tips of my badly bitten fingernails. Instead of accepting the illness and working with it at a reasonable pace I was running a race against a formidable opponent and I could not possibly win. That winter vacation it became very clear to me that I was out of my league in this race. When school was out, I collapsed and could not get out of bed. I lie there wondering if I would ever be able to do anything again. I felt as if I had a ton of rocks sitting on my chest and it was a major effort to remember to brush my teeth. I felt an overwhelming sense of grief, as if I had died, as if nothing would ever be the same. I cried, no sobbed, for what seemed like forever. I felt lost with no way out. I remembered this feeling from when my father died. It was empty and lonely and it made me question whether or not I could go on. I was angry at the sun shining and offended that anyone could laugh in my presence. How dare this happen to me? I was angry at God and I questioned any thing I had believed was spiritual truth. I was in the familiar black hole in my mind and I was feeling physically sick also. I wasn't hit by a bolt of lightening, I had no big aha moment but as the days went by I regained some strength and I began to spend my time thinking about my new diagnosis. Thinking about it is too kind a way to put it. I was brooding about it and drowning in self pity. When I started to look better, my family asked things like, "what's for dinner, where's my shirt" and other normal questions. I didn't want to be helpful. Didn't they know that I have bipolar disorder, that I am too tired to care where your shirt is, I can't make dinner and please leave me alone? Everything they said got on my very last nerve. Couldn't they see I was busy wallowing in my own stuff, that I was consumed by thoughts of myself? Apparently not because they kept asking me to do what I had always done. At some point they wore me down and slowly I tried to do what they asked of me. After a few days it occurred to me that I was not feeling as bad as I had when I was just lying in bed. I was not spending all my time thinking about me and surprisingly that was good. I started to accept that I could feel better. In fact, I was behaving my way back from the depths of despair by making dinner and finding that damn shirt. None of this came from any prescription pad but it was just what I needed.

I had a month off from school and I used that time to figure out how I could reach my goals without sacrificing my health. I decided that I needed to go slower. I needed to prioritize. The dirt behind the refrigerator would have to stay there, I wouldn't iron, I could only make big meals on weekends, and I would have to lower some of my ridiculous standards. For the many years before my diagnosis, all the energy spent on unnecessary projects must have been from manic phases. I was so particular that if I had company I had to make sure that all my closets were organized just in case anyone looked. The truth is that if someone coming over to dinner looks in my closet they deserve to have all the things I've hidden in there including some skeletons fall on them. If I wanted to continue to go to school and to be a good mother and wife, I had to really look at my values and choose what was important. My energy needed to be focused on those things and all the other meaningless actions needed to stop. At first I really thought that I was not doing well if my house wasn't perfect but then I began to see that I had more energy to use to help me complete my goals. Energy has to be rationed. Give your best and most to your family, your work, your friends and slow down on the things that have no lasting meaning. On my tombstone I don't want it written, "she never had dust bunnies." I want to be remembered by the things I've done and the people I have loved. In some ways this new way of thinking was very liberating. It took some of the shoulds and have tos out of my life. For me this was the beginning of acceptance. I could see that I was still a person who could be useful. I could define what I could do and I wasn't less because I had to do less. I could be someone who changed priorities without losing my best qualities. I think we have to know that having bipolar disorder changes our ability to stay on some time lines but it doesn't stop us from creating new ones. Try to look objectively at how you spend your time and cut out stuff that isn't important to make room for the things that will really help you towards recovery. The lesson is that you will have to live with this, but remember, everyone has to live with something. No one has a trouble free life. You can decide to accept this or to fight it. I believe that if you fight it you waste precious time and energy. If you want to continue on the path to your goals, you have to accept the disorder and work with it. Behind all the symptoms there is the person you always were, waiting to get a chance to succeed. Keep remembering that you are a person and not an illness and you will be able to see past the symptoms to determine what you can accomplish. Revel in your uniqueness and use it to create your life.

The eighth and last link is to remain hopeful. Hope is a precious commodity and sometimes it is hard to come by. Without hope all the above links are impossible to use. To keep hope alive appreciate what you are able to do. I figure that as long as I am breathing there is hope that I can do something to change my situation. I may stumble but ultimately I will pick myself up and try again. Don't let anyone tell you that you can't do what is important to you. Remember we are the stream that goes around, under and over rocks that are obstacles to our path. We don't give up and we don't fold. We pace ourselves and we continue to hold onto our vision. Whatever that vision is know that you deserve to make it happen. The key there is that you, with all your supports in place, will be the one to execute the plan. You will be the one to reach the finish line and the medal will belong to you. Whatever you want for yourself can be reality.

Hope is the glue that makes recovery possible. Make it super glue. Hold onto it even when it doesn't seem realistic to do so. Be stubborn on your own behalf. I know that I have great hopes for my own future. I also know that from time to time I will feel hopeless, but when I do I will use the other seven links to help me move forward. Sometimes movement is slow but as long as it is happening we are on the right track.

The natural tendency of the human spirit is to reach for hope. If we don't get in the way with negative thoughts, we will be able to see that. When I was going to school I met a man who had lived through the holocaust. He told his story to our class and I remember feeling that it was a tremendous privilege to see his strength and to learn about his survival. He was only fourteen when he lost both his parents and he had to learn to live on his own. He came to America because he thought he could build a life here and he was able to do so. He had a wonderful wife and five children and many grandchildren. He was thriving in life despite the tragic circumstances of his youth. Just what his parents would have wanted for him. The class cried as he told his story and someone asked what we all were thinking. How did you go on, what made you so strong? He said, "My parents had hopes and dreams for me and when they died it was my job to achieve them. I didn't question whether I could do it, I just believed that I would." I never forgot that story or that quote. We need to hold on to what we want and not abandon our hopes and dreams. If that wonderful man could beat the odds I know we can too. Let yourself hope and find strength in that hope. Use all your tools to thrive, and as you try know that I am trying right along with you.

## Strength-based Assessment Worksheet

1.  What do I like about myself?

2.  What are my strengths?

3.  What do I do best-talents, hobbies, etc.?

4.  What was I doing the last time I was proud of myself?

5.  What characteristics do I value in myself?

6.  What do I deserve in life, because I am a good person?

## Strength-based assessment card

Here is who I really am.

1.

2.

3.

4.

5.

6.

7.

8.

9.

10.

## Goals Work Sheet

1.  What do you value most in your life?

2.  What makes you feel good about yourself when you do it?

3.  What is your passion and how can it add meaning to your life?

4.  How do I want my life to look?

5.  What are my short term goals?

6.  What are my long term goals?

7.  Define the steps to getting there?

**For clients**

1.  What works best for you to improve your life?

2.  What makes life more difficult?

3.  What issues do you see in our treatment systems that don't work? Do you have any suggestions to help change this?

4.  Do you believe that you can achieve your goals and dreams?

5.  How has mental illness changed your philosophy of life?

6.  What is your outlook for the future-positive and negative?

# What is a Person?

A person is a combination
The sum of many parts
One part is personality
A large part is heart
Along comes an illness
That snatches like a thief
The very qualities
That make a person unique
An illness can be defined by words in a book
A person is defined by much more, if you care to look
We have to look deep inside, to the person that's real
In order to help them to think and to feel
A diagnosis is only a label
A small box to keep people in
A person is so much more than his symptoms
Till he sees this, healing can't begin
Doctors and scientists, beware of labels
People can do much more, if we believe they are able
They aren't just symptoms or a disease
Their hearts, minds and spirits are eager to please
They want to live life and do many things
But they need our support and the hope that it brings
We have to look deep inside and try to relate
For when we do the rewards will be great
These people are special and awesomely made
For a person is the sum of many parts
Some personality and a large part heart

# For the Families of Children and Teens—Special Tools

There are many books on the clinical aspects of children and adolescents with bipolar disorder. I would like to offer you practical tips on how to be helpful and just how to live through this experience. In my years working with children and their families I have seen the heartbreak and disappointment felt by both. The children try so hard to control something they don't understand. They are too young to have the advanced coping skills to handle their symptoms. The parents are scared they are not doing the right thing, guilty because their child is so unhappy and perplexed at what to do about it. The emotions and patience of the child and the parents are taxed. Solutions are complex and everyone wants definite answers and cures. It is hard to accept that a five or a ten year old can get this diagnosis and have to deal with it for the rest of their lives. On top of all that, there is intense sadness and constant worry. Sometimes it all seems like too much. In the weekly support groups that I facilitate for these parents I hear their pain. I also run some groups for the children and adolescents and the theme for them is that they just want to be "normal". I cannot bring a cure, but I can offer ways to make this livable, successful and somewhat positive. As a social worker and therapist, I feel it is my job to help people accept what they have and thrive despite it.

The professional community has a hard time diagnosing and treating children and teens because of lack of specific research on medications for them. Psychiatrists don't want to diagnose too young or fail to treat soon enough. I know that parents are always concerned about hearing the diagnosis. My first piece of advice is that you need to look at the child's symptoms on a continuum. Classic depression and mania may not be easy to detect. While an adult may seem extremely sad and anxious, a child may express those feelings as tantrums or anger. This often happens because children have a more difficult time putting their feelings into words. Knowing that children don't always experience the disorder the same way adults do, can keep you from being in denial because their behavior isn't what you would expect for this diagnosis. As a matter of fact, it would be more beneficial to read books that are appropriate for the age of your child so that you will be able to relate to what you all are experiencing. Another thing you can do is learn what the age appropriate milestones are and calculate what your child is capable of by figuring out where they are emotionally. Until a child is stable, they can act younger than their chronological age. While that is frustrating, expecting things from them that they aren't able to do won't bring any positive results. This can also help differentiate symptoms from the normal drama and angst of children and teens.

Children can be diagnosed as having ADD or ADHD first. If treatments for that fail and problems continue or worsen then they will be assessed for bipolar disorder. Sometimes it is difficult to find a psychiatrist or therapist your child is comfortable with. Keep looking until you do because medication and talking are important components of treatment. You can use the questionnaire provided in this book to assess if the professionals are going to be able to work with your needs. There is not always an instant rapport but if you ask those questions you can see if you are all on the same page.

While this sometimes lengthy process is going on, you, the parent, has to live with the day to day behaviors and feelings of your child. It is you that deals with tears, tantrums, frustration with school and phobias. If you look at those behaviors and work on helping change them you will feel more proactive and you won't get caught waiting for a doctor's official diagnosis to begin making things better. You know your child best and there are things that only you can devise to help. A doctor or therapist can make suggestions but they aren't there to implement them. If someone suggests something you know won't work for your child or in your family, feel free to substitute something that fits better. For better or for worse, you are the expert here. It is the family that loves the person enough to keep on going when it seems like giving up is the only answer. I believe that the two main tools for parenting successfully are improvisation and repetition. What worked today may not work tomorrow. Think about your child before this disorder, or any child that doesn't have it, and recognize that children universally change their minds. They like spaghetti today and tomorrow it's disgusting. Pink is their favorite color, no this week it's green. Our children have the same issues on a grander scale. What will calm them down today may not work the next time. They may fluctuate between moods and opinions at warp speed. It is not our job to agree or disagree, just to model good ways to cope. This is a very difficult task, but done in a spirit of improvisation it can work. I was the therapist to an eight year old boy who couldn't seem to control his crying. Sometimes he would cry over what seemed like nothing to the adults. He could cry for over an hour and his parents had all the reactions from sympathetic to ballistic. We had tried a few different things with varying success. One day when the boy came for his session he was in a good mood. We talked for awhile about what his week was like and he was so agreeable that I decided to risk bringing up his crying jags. I asked him how it felt and he was very patient with his explanation. I wanted to know what he thought would be helpful in stopping his crying. He said sometimes he wanted to be held, sometimes he wanted to be left alone, sometimes music calmed him down and so on. I had him make a list of seven options his parents could use to help him if he was upset. He could tell them the number and then they would have a clue what to do. He was very excited to see how they could work as a team to improve this problem. He brought the list to his parents and they agreed to give it a try. The first time he used it he kept repeating," number three," and his parents got the list and did the corresponding action. It worked. He was able to communicate what he needed and they responded. As time went on different options were added and some were taken away. He made a list to take to school to use with his teacher and school social worker. Eventually he was able to make a list for himself of things he could do to prevent the crying jags. None of this is a cure but it made life easier for that little boy, his parents and the school. Our instinctive reactions, anger and annoyance, have to be changed or we won't be able to reach these children. There are many things that can work and we need to stockpile them and tailor them to our child and to the situation.

Every parent has said, "didn't I tell you this a hundred times,". With our children we may need to make it a thousand times and if that doesn't work try a thousand and one. It is tiresome but if they are having difficulty concentrating or having racing thoughts they will not be able to retain what you say. Eventually, I promise you, it will sink in. They may need a system of signals or notes to remind them what is expected of them. I saw a teenage girl who was so frustrated about her mother always correcting her in public. It embarrassed her and made her angry. On the other hand, her parents felt that they couldn't ignore when she made rude or inappropriate comments. Both of them had valid points but being right wasn't solving the problem. We devised a set of signals that would point out a problem behavior in a more private way. Mom would casually clasp her hands, the daughter would try to pay attention to the signal and stop the behavior. This system was modified many times to take into account different situations and growth and maturity. At some point, when the girl was seventeen, the mom used the thumbs up sign, to respond positively to things she did well. Now that was a successful intervention. It was able to convey needed corrections respectfully and it stopped their public arguments. Again, not a cure, but a help.

When kids have continuing problems parents often become conditioned to look for them., to watch more diligently to see what's wrong. Sometimes the kids do that too. We all get so busy being afraid of bad feelings and behaviors that we forget that mixed in there are things that go well, things we do right. Certainly, ten calls a month from school can push everyone's expectations to the negative side, but it isn't every moment of every day that turns out wrong. As parents, we need to take time to catch our kids doing something right. Whatever it is, acknowledging it can start a chain reaction of better choices. When you help your child and someone points it out you want to work harder, continue to help. The children feel this way too. It is hard to have negative feelings inside, criticism wherever you go, and remain positive. No one means for it to be that way, but nevertheless, that's how it becomes. Everything is a fight, a challenge. When I talk to parents about doing strength based assessments about their child, they are so surprised by this novel approach that they are speechless. If I let them think a bit, they are often amazed by the talents and strengths that are still present. The lists can go on for pages and when that happens I just let them do that without interference. When they are done we read them aloud. I ask them to share this list with their child. Then I ask the child to make a list about the parents and share it with them. This exercise generates good feeling and reminds everyone why they love each other. There are assessment sheets at the end of this chapter for you to use. Finding strengths doesn't change deficits but it shows that you have something to work with to make change. People are able to make changes using strengths they already have and that makes the process less overwhelming. As a parent myself, I know how easy it is to beat myself up for mistakes I 've made. I also know that I have tried to do the best I could and putting myself down is never a step on the road to doing it better. If I can find some things I have done right and keep a sense of humor about my mistakes I can continue to try new things without fear. There is no profit in making myself feel bad and everything to gain by focusing on using my strengths to be helpful to my child. It is also a good example of how to make a mistake and learn from it, not let it stop you from making new progress.

All parents know that they need to pick their battles. For parents of kids with bipolar disorder the battles can be different but you still need to prioritize what is important. For me, safety is at the top of the list. When the child is unsafe, nothing else matters. Whether they are threatening to hurt themselves or have already done it, we need to pay attention. Sometimes parents will state that kids are hurting themselves just to get attention. While that may be true, ignoring them will not make them stop. If they are ignored they will often do something more drastic. At the point of the incident your main goal is to insure safety, no matter what means you have to use. Calling 911, taking the child to the hospital, calling for the police are all valid ways of preventing tragedy. When things have calmed down and the crisis is past you need to look at why your child is choosing to get attention in this negative way. Conversations with psychiatrist and therapist are in order. A safety plan and a crisis plan need to be put in place. You can also contract with your child to keep themself safe. If they know that they can call grandma when they are upset, go to the nurses office at school or speak to someone who helps them calm down, they may make better choices. A contract is not a guarantee that your child will stay safe but it is a written document that can remind them how to get help when they need it. Not knowing what to do can make everyone be less effective. If it is common for there to be this kind of situation in your family, planning will be your best defense against a bad outcome. The plan needs to be flexible enough to be able to be implemented in different environments. If issues can arise at school or boy scouts, the adults who have responsibility for your child's safety need to be included in the plan.

One of the biggest battles parents and kids have is over school attendance and homework. School is important but if your child is feeling mentally unwell, you need to help them get healthy first. A child who is anxious, depressed, confused, scared and can't concentrate won't be able to tolerate the demands of school. If your child is feeling like that, aggressive intervention is needed. When parents bring kids to me that are failing in school I try to get to the bottom of what is going on in class. Is the medication making them too tired? Are they having difficulty understanding the work? What are they thinking about in class? There are so many questions to ask and sometimes the answers are unclear. The child doesn't know how to explain what is going on or just doesn't know. With help from your team of professionals you need to look at options. Is classification for special education necessary to get additional help for your child? Is your child in need of a medication change? All of these issues need to be looked at as soon as the problem arises. There are often many steps needed to get the child to go to school and succeed there. Show your child that you take their difficulties seriously by acting early. The longer it goes on, the harder it is for the child to picture themself doing well in school. The fear and anxiety needs to be dealt with the same way as you would any physically obvious illness. No one would let their child sit at home with a broken arm, hoping it would heal without medical intervention. The same is true here. This is the place that your firm belief that your child has a biologically based brain disorder will push you to seek help.

I know that it is a tough situation because it is part of your responsibility as a parent to educate them. Social services can get involved if your child misses too much school. By the way, when talking to the child, trying to get them to be part of the solution, I frequently remind them that it is the law that they attend school. While we are working on solutions I remind them that not working this out will mean that there can be consequences in many areas of their life. I also try to work with the schools to come up with options that individualize the plan for a specific child. Cookie cutter answers may not help, but I have worked with many schools and families to put together innovative plans that do work. I know it is hard not to focus on the work they are missing. I can reassure you that when they are feeling better they will be able to work better and catch up. In the course of a lifetime no one checks to see if you were eight or ten when you learned how to multiply. The bottom line is that even though their time line may be different, they can still learn what they need to know.

The last thing that I want to address is being consistent and providing structure. People with bipolar disorders do well when they have a good plan, a schedule they can depend on. I know that life isn't always consistent and there is a lesson to be learned in having the ability to be flexible, but putting together some times and activities that remain stable is really helpful. Bedtime rituals, reading together, breakfast on Sunday, all are things that put positive boundaries in kids lives. These children have so many unpredictable feelings and emotions that they need to have something that they can count on. If most of their life has a routine, they will have more energy to rally when things are less stable. As parents, we need to maintain some rules and boundaries at home that will be an example of how to successfully handle situations in other places. When I am working with children and teens I find that they are thrown by changes in weather, holidays, vacations, and a new schedule at school. These seem like normal things to others but not to them. We can't protect them from change but we can prepare them for it. I have had endless conversations in therapy sessions about how to act on vacation, what to do in different places and situations. If you can discuss these situations before they happen you can define the conditions and expectations. Kids may feel more comfortable and confident that they can handle it if they are prepared. Remember, success in one area may help their self esteem so that they can succeed in multiple areas of their lives. It all comes down to supporting them in ways that will help them feel capable.

There are so many good books to read on this subject and I encourage you to read them. Take what works for you and leave the rest. One thing that I know is that to raise these wonderful and challenging children, you need to get support for yourself. A parent support group allows you to speak to others who know what you are going through. They may have great ideas that have worked for them that you can use. At the very least, they will listen and empathize. They can give you advice on how to advocate for your child and support while doing it. In a good support group you can feel comfortable crying, laughing and questioning. It is one place where your situation is not unique and you won't be judged. The last thing I want you to know is that you need to take care of yourself. You are doing the best that you can and striving to do better. Give yourself credit. Don't underestimate the profound effect your love and support will have on this child you love. When it doesn't seem like it's working remember that raising these children is a marathon not a sprint. Focus on your strengths and know that you and your family will get through this.

# Questions To Ask When Choosing A Professional

1.  Have you treated many people with bipolar disorder?

2.  What is the course of treatment?

3.  How effective do you think this treatment will be?

4.  Will you get to know me before you give me medication?

5.  Can you take the time to explain about my illness, treatment, and medication?

6.  Do you have backup coverage when you are not available?

7.  How much time will each session be?

8.  How can I reach you in a crisis?

9.  What is your philosophy about good outcomes for people with bipolar disorder?

10. Will you help me find ways to manage my symptoms?

## Strength Based Assessment (For the Parents)

1. What brings you joy about your child?

2. What are your child's strengths and talents?

## Strength Based Assessment (For the Child/Teen)

1. What are the things I do best?

2. What are my talents?

3. What qualities do I like about myself as a person? (Feel free to use a second page)

# For the Families—Strategies
# For Life

Families are often forgotten in the daily struggle to help the person with the diagnosis. They are too busy finding the treatments, making the calls, meeting their normal life demands to pay attention to the effect bipolar disorder has had on their lives. I know, from listening to many parents, siblings, spouses and friends that their lives have been profoundly changed, but no one seems to notice. Their reactions are similar to their family member's reactions. They are sad and grieving, scared and lost, determined and panicked and often without help. I know that many families get the diagnosis but not much additional information. Sometimes they aren't connected to support groups or know anyone else who is going through similar issues. There is fear, guilt, shame and isolation. People say that you should get a grip, it isn't you who has the disorder. Well they would be wrong. When a family member has a mental illness, the whole family has to deal with it. It can feel like you are on a fast roller coaster ride going up and down, except you don't remember buying the ticket. The person with the disorder has some clue about how they feel but you are left not knowing. A person with whom you had a good and close relationship can suddenly be withdrawn and distant. You wonder if it was something you did or said. They are locked away somewhere and you don't have the key. You want to help but all the ways you related before don't work any more. What can you do and how can you cope?

I remember that my mother's moods always left me confused. I would try lots of different things to cheer her up but nothing worked. I didn't know that what she was feeling was definitely not my fault. I want family members to know this first and foremost, it is NOT your fault. There is nothing that you have said, done, neglected to say or do that makes you responsible for the pain your loved one is going through. Even if, after extensive research you come to the conclusion that the genes causing the illness came from your side of the family, you are still not at fault. Given the choice, you would have chosen only good things for this person. Bipolar disorder can be a hard reality but it can only be blamed on biology. The person has the genes and the chemical imbalance that causes their symptoms. You couldn't, wouldn't and haven't done anything to cause this. That needs to be clear before you can go on to be helpful to your family member and get on with your own life. Please know that you have a right to all your feelings—the good, the bad and the ugly. It is difficult to be in the trenches every day trying to help and never knowing if you are doing the right thing. The families are the ones who are there after five and on the weekends. They may feel like giving up but they don't have the luxury of closing the case or referring them to someone else. We wouldn't have chosen this for our loved one but the people who have the bipolar disorder weren't given a choice either. They drew that card and now they have to figure out the rules of a new game. Although it is difficult, I know that people can negotiate their way through the complexities of being a family member and come out on the other side. If the person you are dealing with is over the age of eighteen you often have to sit back and watch them struggle because they have the legal right to do just that. It is painful, especially if you can see things clearer because you are not struggling with symptoms of depression or mania. I have run hundreds of support groups, counseled parents, siblings, husbands, wives and friends and all my suggestions are based on the wisdom I get from them and on methods that have been tried with some success. Each family will need to find it's own way but if I can shed some light I am more than happy to do so. I believe that families are courageous, caring and persistent. They get less credit and more blame than they deserve. I want to try to offer compassionate ways to live with and among this illness without losing who you are. Families try so hard and they care so much. Their hearts are broken and their dreams are crushed but they still endeavor to know more, do more and they follow any lead that could possibly lead to relief for the person who is lucky enough to be loved by them . It is sometimes thankless and endless, but I am here to tell you that it is not fruitless. My successes have been won on the backs of my family and friends support. I would be unable to persevere without their love and encouragement. I have followed my own advice and done my best to be as mentally healthy as possible, but when I need them, they are there and I am grateful. The people you love are still inside even if it's hard to see them through the cloud of symptoms. They need you to believe in them and to hold the hope of their recovery when it is lost to them. I hope to offer you practical tips that will enable you to conserve your strength for times when you can be helpful. Take some of it or all of it, add to it and subtract from it, but make it your own because it will help bring order to the chaos.

The first thing that I want to cover is that you are in this for the long haul so you can't let yourself get exhausted by the everyday drama. Try not to engage in battles that don't affect the quality of your life. Moods that are not violent can be ignored and sometimes giving someone space is the best solution that yields the quickest results. Some examples of situations that are annoying but not important enough for you to lose sleep over are, the family member sleeping too much, not exercising, dressing poorly, gaining weight. These can all be upsetting but they are not tragic and they are part of the slow recovery process or symptoms of the illness. This is the time when you remember that when they feel better they will be more open and able to participate in life. You can have a hundred conversations about this and they may want to do what you say, but at that time they may not be well enough to follow through. What can be helpful is to let them know that you are going for a walk, getting up at eight, or willing to do some laundry with them. You are opening a door for them but not trying to force them to walk in. It is difficult, but here is one area where it is clear that you can want them to be better, with all of your heart, but you can't make it happen.

Make suggestions, but don't micro manage situations that will work out on their own with time. It is good to express confidence in their ability to be productive. It's a balancing act between expecting too much from them too soon after a bad episode and not giving them enough credit or allowing them space to do what they can. You love them and you want them to progress but you have to keep a check on whether your expectations are reasonable. If they have had a recent hospitalization or a serious bout of depression, they will know when they are capable of moving on and trying new things. No one wants to add pressure to an already difficult situation but it's hard not to want them to return to their functional selves. The trick here is to believe and know that they need to heal and that they will heal. Take your cues from them, but be confident that with your support they will make progress.

Maya Angelou has said," People do well when they can, and when they can do better, they do better." Daily living with someone with bipolar disorder isn't easy or smooth. Sometimes, it just doesn't flow. As their families you need to remember that they didn't choose to have this and it is very hard for them. We need to be patient and believe that with time, medication, better coping skills and therapy they will be able to do better. Both family and the person with the illness want the same thing. For this to be workable, patience is the key. During my years working at the community residence I saw many people who couldn't accomplish even simple tasks, like laundry or vacuuming, when they started to live there but within a year or two they had learned enough to live on their own successfully. If independence is your goal, patience is your mantra.

A very important point to consider is how much influence this illness has had on the way you live your life. The person with the illness cannot and should not dominate everything a family does. Other people matter and need to be allowed to continue doing normal things. Sometimes it is hard for them to be in a crowd or attend family functions, don't try to force them to do things they aren't comfortable with. When they are feeling better, they will want to be part of general life again. Take the lead from them but don't be led by them. When I have been depressed I have had hard times doing some social things because it takes all my energy to accomplish the required daily living tasks. When the depression lifts, I can't wait to get back to the fun, family activities. People who are symptomatic often feel that they won't be good company, or that people will question them, or that they sound dumb when they speak. They aren't enjoying being with themselves and they don't believe anyone would want to be with them. However, the family still needs to do things they enjoy. You wish the person would do them with you, but they aren't ready to. The intention of the family is that, "maybe if she/he goes out he will feel better." This is where you have to stop trying to fix what you can't. You going on with your life and regular activities allows the person to have time and space to heal and alleviates the guilt they feel when everything comes to a halt because of their fluctuating moods.

Everyone makes mistakes. It is part of the human condition. Family members cannot protect their loved ones from making mistakes or getting hurt. They have the right to make mistakes, try different things and fail at it or get hurt by the outcome of it. I have had five different careers with some success in each one. At the end of each, sometimes, what I learned was that what I had been so sure I wanted, wasn't really it. The attitude that you want to promote is one where they can appreciate what they learn from experiences, both successful and not so successful. It is not helpful to create an atmosphere that is so far from reality that they have no opportunity to develop their resiliency. I have had many clients who were never encouraged to try things for fear of how they would react if it didn't work out. In these instances, no one considered the possibility that it could be great for them, they could have experiences that made them feel useful and could connect them to meaningful ways to live their lives. A family's job, difficult as it may be is to love, support and encourage. Everything that your relative says may seem impossible and if it is they will find that out. If you have stood by them they will be more likely to allow you to help them and suggest things to them. They take the chance that they will fail if they try, but if they never try they face the certainty of a failed life. The bottom line is that if they need you to help them you are there and they know that you love them enough to believe in their abilities.

Coping skills are essential to live. We all develop them and use them if they work for us. Your family member needs to do this and you need to allow them to be able to. I acknowledge that you probably have the answers, the solutions and the desire to save them from this painful, often slow process. Although it may be difficult to restrain yourself, you need to let them discover the answers on their own. If they learn it that way, it will be their knowledge to use in life. If you solve all my problems I have no reason to be independent. Statements like, "That won't work, do it this way" only serve to undermine their efforts to make good decisions. Saying, "I don't know if that will work but if you think it will, give it a try" or "I have confidence that you can figure it out" will give them the opportunity to feel supported as they try new things. The time will come when, because you have been supportive, you get to voice an opinion about what has worked for you. Show confidence in their ability to work things out and lead by example. They have lived with you and they know how you do things so trust that they will use what they have already learned from you. When I have been depressed I think I can do nothing, when I am manic I think I can do everything. Neither is true. What has worked for me is my husband's unwavering belief that I will be able to figure it out.

Having a mental illness does not excuse rude, violent or inappropriate behavior. A good friend of mine had a son who had schizophrenia and she would always say to him, "Appropriate is appropriate" She refused to accept from him what she wouldn't accept from other people. An entire family should not be walking on egg shells to accommodate the bad behavior of one person. There is a definite difference between symptoms and just plain rudeness. A person who is depressed may not be eloquent in their conversation but they still know that cursing out mom is wrong. Do not excuse this because it enables them to continue it. Help them find ways to express themselves but be clear about where the line is between expressing a feeling and being abusive. If you allow them to be this way at home it will carry over to other parts of their life and will affect their ability to maintain relationships and hold jobs. Not allowing this behavior teaches personal responsibility. This is something I have learned in my work as a case manager for children with serious emotional and behavioral difficulties. It also comes into play when I teach parenting classes. You can have excuses such as, he's just tired, his meds are not working, the poor thing she just can't help herself, or you can use the times when they are inappropriate to show them what is acceptable. They can trade in, "You SOB", for "I am upset now and I need time to cool down."

Sometimes you just become tired by the endless behaviors that are annoying, frustrating and hurtful to you. It is okay for you to withdraw, take time to gather your thoughts and then address what was said, but it isn't okay to accept bad behavior or to ignore it. When addressing it you need to try to stay calm and just state how you feel and what you will and won't tolerate. Arguing and confronting will only continue the incident and escalate the behaviors. Even when your head feels about to explode you will feel better if you don't engage in the conversation in a negative way. Saying, "I hate you, you are an idiot, selfish and ungrateful," may be valid comments but I promise you they won't be helpful and you will feel bad later. In these situations I do what I call, "blank talking." It is responding in a way that validates how upset the person is and gives voice to their feelings without agreeing with them. I will share with you two stories that will give you some idea how it works. In the first situation there is a girl who continuously tells her mother what a bad mother she has been. She says that mom didn't come to her track meets and doesn't care about her. She thinks mom loves her siblings more than her. This has become a daily conversation and the mom is feeling very defensive about her parenting. Mom has yelled at the girl, tried to remind her of all the good times they have had together, bought her sappy cards hoping for a Hallmark cure and even gone as far as dragging out all the family pictures as proof that they have had fun and that she is a good mother. The girl is not persuaded. Her perceptions of her childhood remain the same. I spoke to the mother and we devised a new strategy. When the daughter starts the conversation, the mother is to cut her off at the pass by saying, "It must be very hard to feel that way." She is not to argue and she can continue, in a calm voice, to repeat that previous statement. That statement validates the girl's feelings but does not concede agreement. After a few minutes the mom can say, "I understand that you are upset but I won't have that conversation with you anymore because it is upsetting to me." This shows that illness does not give them carte blanch to hurt others feelings. She repeated this scenario with her daughter quite a few times and the girl stopped trying to engage her mother in this specific conversation because she couldn't get the response she desired. The result is that even if the daughter hasn't changed her feelings and opinions, she knows that mom will not listen to her on this subject. At that point the mom needs to find a friend or a support group where she can talk about how she feels and be validated and applauded for not engaging in another endless and fruitless argument.

The second situation happened when I was an intensive case manager for children with serious emotional disabilities. As the observer in the family I would often see that when the children would tantrum, the parents would become so frustrated and even afraid that they would give in. The child would think he had won, but the reality of it is that if the parent doesn't maintain the position of leader, nobody wins. I had been working on this with the family but they were finding it very hard to outlast him and maintain their positions when he was upset. It was holiday time and we had decided that I would take him shopping to get gifts for his family. We clearly discussed what we would be doing before we left. We only had enough money for him to buy presents for his mother, father and sister. We would not be buying him anything that day but at the end of the shopping we would go to McDonalds for lunch. He agreed and we went to the local Walmart. He chose nice presents for his family and I gave him much positive feedback about his choices, how generous he was being and how much everyone would appreciate his thoughtfulness. I thought we were home free until we passed a toy that he felt he had to have. He was expressing his need for this toy as if it was equivalent to his need for air. I said that I understood that he wanted it and sometimes it was hard not to get what you want, but I repeated our agreement for this trip, reminding him about going to lunch after we left the store. He was not impressed by anything I said and he began to scream, "you will buy me this toy, I hate you, you're mean." repeatedly. As he was doing this people started to stare, become annoyed even offer suggestions. What I wanted most at this point was to be wearing a T-shirt that said, "this boy is not my son." At that moment it was perfectly clear to me why the mom always gave in. It was, in fact, tempting for me to give in. Somewhere inside me I knew that someone had to show him that he wasn't in charge, that saying no was something he would have to deal with. For forty-five minutes with many onlookers I continued to say," I know that you want that but we won't be getting it, and several other variations of that sentence. He couldn't break me even though inside myself I was thinking of ways to quit my job by pinning a note on this boys shirt and calling my boss to come pick him up. He finally became tired and he calmed down enough to pay for the things and leave the store, much to the relief of the cashiers and customers. When I brought him home, he proceeded to tell his mom about what had occurred from his point of view. She couldn't believe that I hadn't given in to his demands. I worked with her on the blank talking method and she certainly used it with some success. The bottom line is I didn't insult him or call him names, I just didn't let him get his way and he learned that the world didn't end just because someone said no. I took him out many times after that and we never had a repeat performance. I am by no means suggesting that this is easy but it is necessary for your survival to be able to remain in control during these types of interactions so that you don't escalate them or say and do things you will regret later.

Violence is never to be accepted because no matter how sorry someone is it doesn't erase the incident from your mind. If your relative really hurts you how will you trust them again and how will they live with themselves. You need to have a safety plan and you have to be willing to use it. Calling 911 is difficult but no less difficult than losing your relationship with someone you love. A hospitalization may be needed, a plan to deescalate may be used, but never compromise on safety. Each family has to have ownership of a part of the safety plan so that they can feel helpful if a crisis occurs. Who makes the phone calls, who is most likely to be able to calm the person down, what hospital takes your insurance, who goes to the hospital and who helps with the assessment or admission. Planning will alleviate some of the chaos and the family members can feel useful. Not planning won't keep a crisis from happening. You are the one who sets the standard and you are the one who makes the boundaries. Model calm and organized behavior and then have a friend or family member on hand with a strong shoulder for a good cry when the crisis is past.

You are the keeper of the hope. When our loved ones cannot see that hope we need to continue to believe in their ability to recover. It was so important to me that my family and friends stood with me and encouraged me to reach my goals. On days when I felt that I could never be who I used to be or grow to be who I wanted to be, they believed that I could. They saw me as I was and while it was upsetting that I wasn't okay at that moment, they didn't lose the perspective of my recovery. They were positive when I was uncertain and it was a gift that is priceless. Recovery can be slow but it is extremely possible. That you can see the person you love and encourage them by bringing out the qualities that you know are in them is the best thing you can do. Mental illness makes family members feel powerless but I am telling you that it is your contribution of support, compassion, humor and love that make the road to recovery easier to travel.

Finally, please take care of yourself. You becoming sick will not make your relative well. It will only rob you of living your best life. Physically, emotionally and spiritually, make it a point to find out how to feel the best you can. Get support, do normal things, enjoy friends and find something that offers you peace. To be helpful to your family member you need to be in good shape. You have the right to have fun, laugh, travel and reach your own goals. Reward your compassion with the knowledge that your life is important too. I want you to remember that once you have done all you can, you have to find rest knowing that your loved one has to do their part. We would take this illness away if we could but we can't. For there to be any kind of victory we need to work with the whole team, professionals, family members and the person with the bipolar disorder. You are not the "team" just an important part of it.

## For the families

1. What works best for you in improving your life?

2. What makes life more difficult?

3. What issues are complicated by the system? Any suggestions for change?

4. Do you believe that you can achieve peace and acceptance?

5. How has your family member's illness changed your philosophy of life?

# For the Professional

I write this to you as a professional social worker who appreciates the difficulties we all face in our work. No one comes to us because things are good in their lives. People want us to fix it and some are not patient at all. Insurance has become such a big problem that it often seems as if benefits direct practice—a totally backward system. Our hours are long, our boundaries are stretched and we often experience vicarious trauma from all the heart breaking stories we hear. Yet, for me, there is nothing else I would rather do. I have grown and changed over the years of my career in experience and expertise, but I have never lost my enthusiasm for my work. In the beginning I wanted to bring everyone home and just make them soup and care for them. I became way too involved in their lives and the outcomes of their choices. I had to learn and relearn the boundaries. It was always my empathy and compassion that drove my work but as I gained knowledge and clinical experience, I could see that sometimes you have to make difficult choices in the quest to help. It is not always beneficial to be "nice" and not ask the hard questions. My expectations have changed. I thought, possibly in a grandiose way, that I could change peoples lives, with or without their consent. In the beginning I was often the girl scout taking the elderly lady across the street even when it was clear that she didn't want to go. I know that I thought that the treatment plan was done by me, not in collaboration with my client. I think I really believed I knew what was best. When I think of that I can see it as an immaturity in my professional vision. Now I really want to empower my clients to make good, independent choices in their lives. It is not what I do or say, but how they use it in their lives. They get the credit for wanting to change and for doing all the hard work to get there. I see myself as an agent of change and sometimes a cheerleader and a coach. I always thought of myself as a solution—come to me, talk about it, feel better. Now I see that I can only be a small part of their journey. While I am working with them I will give them one hundred per cent, but I know that what I say and do may or may not alter the way they think and live. I am able to be kind to myself if people don't progress because I know that I give it my best shot. I try to remain nonjudgmental and accepting. I try to start where they are and pace myself according to where they want to go. I have decided not to work harder than my clients and I use that insight to guide my clinical interventions. At the start of my career, my commitment was endless and I would go to any lengths to get results. Now, I check the level of my commitment by continuing to expect myself to go the extra mile, but not to hang on for the length of a turnpike.

The professionals that I have met, been treated by and worked with, are people of integrity and dedication. I have seen my share of those who are burned out, discouraged, but I feel that they are in the minority. My heart goes out to them because they must be disappointed in themselves. They have tried, perhaps too hard for too long, and have nothing left to give. I hope and pray that I can avoid feeling that way. It is my goal to stay interested in and excited by the work. If I can't feel that way, I hope I have the good grace and sense of self preservation to do something else. I have learned that it is important to take really good care of myself. I need to keep those parts of me that are not involved in my work alive. I vacation regularly, because I believe that people can be fine without me. I have a hobby. I make jewelry in my spare time and that has become a welcome and creative diversion from worrying about my clients. I also appreciate time with my family and friends and I put work issues behind mental barriers so as not to interfere with these occasions. I know that the intensity of our work needs to be balanced by a commitment to family, friends, relaxation and fun. It is because we give so much, so willingly, that we have to decide to accept help when we need it. It is a gift for others when we can allow them to feel that they have positively affected our lives. I always tell my clients how much I appreciate what I have learned from them. All the book knowledge in the world doesn't approach what I have learned from my work experiences. I am open to any new research and techniques and I try to keep up with my reading, but the real learning is from doing the work. I always say that I take what I know and adapt it to my own style, and I do plenty of mixing and matching of theories to get results.

As professionals we need to support each other and find forums to talk together. I learn so much by listening to how other people handle different clinical situations. I appreciate all the hard work I see done by all of us and I think that sometimes we are too hard on ourselves. Instead of seeing ten successes, we see the one that didn't go well. I try to maintain a belief in the integrity of my intentions and an understanding that I will not always be able to help. I have made some good associations with other professionals and I know when to refer patients to someone who is a better fit.

I guess that one of the most difficult principles to maintain is to see each person as an individual. They may have symptoms that are common to their disorder, but no two people are identical. They will not have the same reactions to treatment so the cookie cutter approach won't work. We need to get to know the person and their unique story. That is what keeps it interesting for me. I am fascinated with the variety of stories and circumstances. I really enjoy the problem solving aspect of my work. Good results thrill me but the persistence and patience of the clients is what encourages me to keep trying. I try to be creative using imagery, music, art and journaling and any other idea that might work. I am amazed by the insights of my clients when I find the right means for them to express them. I want to work as part of a treatment team to give a well-rounded plan that helps the client feel supported enough to achieve whatever they define as success.

In closing, for the professionals that have helped and believed in me, I have endless gratitude. For the ones that I have worked with, I am thankful for their knowledge, support and encouragement. I look at all you do and know that I am proud to be a part of our profession. I hope that you all appreciate your dedication and zest for your work and know that you make a difference in people's lives.

## For the professional

1. What are the roadblocks to best practice methods?

2. What are the systems issues?

3. What encourages you to overcome roadblocks and system issues?

4. What do you do for clients and families that promotes positive change?

978-0-595-43008-

0-595-43008-2